A HERITAGE OF HYMNS

A HERITAGE OF HYMNS

An Exploration of Music and Religion, Music and Our Hymns, and the Stories of Hymns and Hymn Writers of the Restoration Movement

Edited by Richard Clothier

Herald Publishing House
Independence, Missouri

© 1996
Herald Publishing House
Independence, Missouri

Printed in the United States of America

Library of Congress Cataloging-in-Publication Data
Clothier, Richard.
    A heritage of hymns: an exploration of music and religion, music and our hymns, and the stories of hymns and hymn writers of the Restoration movement/Richard Clothier.
    p. cm.
    ISBN 978-0-8309-0737-3
    1. Reorganized Church of Jesus Christ of Latter Day Saints—Hymns—History and criticism. 2. Hymns, English—United States—History and criticism. 3. Mormon Church—Hymns—History and critiicsm. 1. Title
BV437.R56C57   1996   96-8803
264'.09302—dc20   CIP

00 99 98 97 96   1 2 3 4 5

For all the Saints

Table of Contents

Introduction 9
Prelude 11
Part I: The Language of the Spirit 15
Part II: Music and Our Hymns 29
          Beyond the Hymnal 53
Part III: Hymns of the Restoration 67
Postlude 163
Index of Authors and Translators, Part III 165
Index of Composers and Arrangers, Part III 167

Introduction

Words © 1972 by Hope Publishing Company of Carol Stream, IL 60188. All rights reserved. Used by permission.

Prelude

My love affair with hymns began when I was a child. My father served as pastor of several congregations in Independence, Missouri, and the family made it a practice to be at church whenever the doors were open. At that early age, I was not always interested in what was being said, but I do remember enjoying the hymn singing. Having begun piano lessons at age five, I looked forward eagerly to the time when I could manage to make my way at the keyboard through even the shortest and simplest numbers from the *Saints' Hymnal*. When that time came, a sympathetic music director and an understanding junior pastor at Spring Branch Congregation believed that my musical development was more important than hearing all the right notes, and encouraged me in the responsibility of playing the piano for junior church services week in and week out.

Over the years a great many hymns have become like good friends to me. And I never fail to thrill when I discover a new hymn that expresses profound thoughts with eloquent grace and beauty. Frequently I have wondered, during periods of worship and song, how many of those assembled are aware of the treasures they hold in their hands and proclaim with their voices.

Recently, as I was writing material for a course to be taught at Graceland College, I decided to incorporate a few hymns from the current hymnal of the RLDS Church, *Hymns of the Saints* (Herald House, 1981). The course was an attempt to make connections between music and religion, with particular emphasis on developing an increased understanding and appreciation of the musical art; some of this material has been incorporated into the first two parts of this book. I had selected several hymns with tunes that had been written during various periods of musical history and planned to discuss these as an introduction to the study of those time periods.

Somewhere during the process of investigating the background of these hymns, it occurred to me that, while there are a number of published commentaries on general Christian hymns, there is not much information available about contemporary RLDS hymns. I remembered how much I had valued Roy Cheville's book about Latter Day Saint hymns, *They Sang of the Restoration*, a work no longer in print. So, for my own benefit and potentially that of my college class, I decided to write to the living authors and composers of new RLDS hymns in *Hymns of the Saints* (I use the abbreviation *HS* and specific hymn numbers throughout the rest of this book) to solicit comments about their hymns and about themselves as well.

In a very short time I received so many interesting responses that I began to realize that what I was collecting deserved to be treated more extensively and shared more widely than I had originally planned. And as I went on to search out the stories of hymns and hymn writers of previous generations, I found myself gaining a new appreciation of the unique heritage that is a part of the fellowship of the church. This is what I have tried to share in the commentary on RLDS hymns that forms Part III, the heart of this book.

Much of this writing was done while spending a sabbatical semester in England, on leave from Graceland College. In that setting, as I worked through the stories of these hymns, I could not help but notice how many of them came from the pens of individuals who had either attended Graceland College or had roots in England—and in some cases both. To me this seemed a testimony of the leading role that has been played in the church's history by a dedicated college and also by the traditions of great hymnody and eloquent speech expressed in the culture of the British Isles.

In my comments on *HS* 314, I have remarked that the hymnals of the church have served to both reflect and foster the changing beliefs of the movement through the years. This idea is echoed by several of the RLDS hymn writers discussed in Part III. An apt example is the comment of Kenneth McLaughlin, noted with the discussion of *HS* 365, that "hymn texts are one of the most important sources of theological instruction in our faith community." Similarly, another student of hymns, Roy Oakman of Enfield, England, has said he believes that because of the absence of an official creed for the RLDS Church, the hymns of the church have served over the years to fill that role and have thus been vital in expressing and shaping the theology of the body.

There are many expressions in our hymns of current beliefs and concepts important to the faith journey we share. A listing of these would be lengthy but would certainly include contemporary concepts of Zion (*HS* 314), the nature of scripture (*HS* 299 and 306), the source of truth in both science and religion (*HS* 298), foundational beliefs of the Restoration (*HS* 398), and even the relationship between life and death itself (*HS* 150).

It is my hope that through the following pages the reader will gain new insights and also catch something of the spirit of those who have given us, through song, the expressions of their deepest faith, their innermost desires, and their fondest dreams. Clearly the convictions and beliefs of a people of faith are not only *expressed* but *molded* by the songs they sing. Thus are the hymns of a movement central and vital to the understanding of its past as well as the hopes for its future.

Richard Clothier

PART ONE

The Language of the Spirit

Why should Feeling ever speak,
When thou canst breathe her soul so well?
—Thomas Moore, "On Music"

Why do we sing hymns? For as long as anyone knows, singing has been a natural part of life and of worship. What is so special about the art of song? Why do so many people, including those who do not consider themselves artistic or musical, join so freely in this particular art? The answers to those questions involve qualities unique to the art of music. For this is an art, so natural and yet so complex, that communicates human emotions in a particular and peculiar way. We sing because we have discovered that through music we are able to impart and receive the deepest of expressions and the most penetrating of revelations.

Music as Expression

They are just three words: "I love you." But they are probably the most often repeated words in human history, in every language known to civilization. They are also words that have most often found their way into music because, long ago, people in love realized that when words alone are not sufficient to express the deepest passions of the heart, music emerges.

For this reason, songs of love and praise, whether of a beloved person or a divine being, account for a large portion of the music of humankind. Ballads of romantic love, from a multitude of styles, nations, and eras, are among the most popular of all musical expressions. Songs of praise and worship of Divinity make up a significant part of the heritage of many cultures. There is no better way to express joy, sorrow, pain, awe, pity, or devotion than through the skillful use of melody, rhythm, and harmony. At its best, music has the power to move people to the depths of their beings.

Why does music have these unique qualities? The answer lies in music itself, and in what it can and cannot do. Melody, harmony, rhythm, and tone color can combine magically to transport one to another dimension, to create an atmosphere, mood, or emotional state almost instantaneously. Music (without words) is an abstract art form—it cannot tell a story or paint a picture. What it does best is reach into the depths of human experience and communicate the most strongly felt emotions, those that are beyond words to express. This is the level where we really live; it is the realm of the human soul. The language of musical expression is not the language of words or of any other form of utterance. It is none other than the language of the spirit.

The art of music, however, has always been closely associated with words. When we sing, we are really engaging a unique combination of two arts. Music alone, pure music, is essentially instrumental. When this pure music is combined with verbal expression as a vocal art, another level is reached. Here the more specific expressions of words are combined with the spiritual expressions of music, and a dual art form results that can enhance, intensify, and illuminate a text, and minister to the very soul. Thus, instead of just saying, "I love you," it can be much more effective and moving to sing it. That is why humankind has turned to music when there is no other way to share the depths yearning to be expressed. When that love is too deep for words, that longing too intense, that sorrow beyond description, or that joy unspeakable, there is music.

While writing this book I had the opportunity to witness the rejoicing of a nation as the people of Britain commemorated the fiftieth anniversary of Victory in Europe day—VE day. This, of course, was the day the Nazi forces surrendered to the Allies, bringing to an end a major portion of the most horrific conflict in human history. On this anniversary, a crowd of hundreds of thousands had massed outside Buckingham Palace, and they were singing with an enthusiasm rarely found in today's society. Scarcely a dry eye could be found in that multitude. On the surface, the songs they sang were simple; one, for example, was about bluebirds. How could this little song have such an enormous emotional impact on all those people?

The answer to that question is to be found in the deeper meaning of the words, in the heartfelt melody that conveys them, and in the tremendous associations that song has for those who sang it. Fifty years ago was a time that was at once Britain's darkest hour and its finest one. After most of Europe had given in to the Nazi dictator, this island nation, despite heavy damage and loss of life, stood alone in its defiance of the forces of fascism. The courage of the people was buoyed up in those days by their pride, their leaders, their love of freedom, and their traditions, not the least of which was their heritage of singing. These all came together in that little song about bluebirds; in fact, it is really not about birds at all but about faith. It was a song of hope for a better world, where children would no longer have to flee the cities, where homes would no longer be destroyed, where food would not have to be rationed, where young men and women could look forward to growing old, and where the song of birds would be heard again throughout the land: "There'll be bluebirds over the white cliffs of Dover, tomorrow, when the world is free."

The incalculable power of heartfelt words meeting poignant music in that simple song, and others like it, gave a people the strength to fight on, to the death if need be, to reclaim a future for themselves and their children. Such is the cry of the human spirit in song.

Music as Revelation

The spiritual communication music makes possible allows not only for the expression but also the reception of truth. Experiencing music at its best can indeed be a revelatory experience. Perhaps this concept can be illustrated by a personal testimony.

From my teenage years, I can recall several penetrating experiences with what were often called the "gifts of the Spirit." These were, by and large, manifestations of advice and counsel given to a particular group by a minister speaking in the first person in the name of Divinity. Now, after many years, I do not remember much of what was said on these occasions, but the electric feeling and the overwhelming sense of sacredness and "rightness" were unforgettable. It was the knowledge that I was in the midst of something quite extraordinary, beyond and above most of the experiences life has to offer.

During these same years I remember another experience that had a very comparable effect on my young life. It was just as profound and just as holy, except that it did not take place in a church building or a reunion tent or in a youth campfire setting, but rather at a concert hall. Just as I had been immersed in religious activities as a teenager, I had also been involved in music, particularly through participation in various bands and orchestras. I had attended professional concerts before, but never by one of the world's great orchestras, until the day the Philadelphia Orchestra came to Kansas City.

Although I have since had the privilege of hearing many outstanding musical performances, I will never forget the experience that night in the old Kansas City Music Hall. I had never imagined that any music could be so inspiring, so enthralling, so perfect, so powerful, and so moving. Just as I do not remember what was said in the other "mountaintop" experiences of my youth, neither do I remember what the

Philadelphians played, but I will never forget the spirit of that performance. And I clearly remember talking with one of my close friends afterward and observing that that experience was essentially the same as the other "gifts of the Spirit" we had witnessed through the fellowship of the church. For through both experiences there came the powerful sense of truth and rightness, and the knowledge that we were in the midst of something powerful and transcendent.

Peter Schaffer, in his play *Amadeus*, has the court composer Salieri exclaim when he hears for the first time the music of the young Mozart, "I thought I had heard the voice of God." There are many ways through which we can experience the "voice" of Divinity. Certainly one of these is music, which, in its best moments, can speak with this kind of power. In this profound art we have an important channel through which we can be privileged to sense the very heart of God opening to us, saying, "Here for you is a glimpse of what I am like."

As one listens with greater perception to the way melody, harmony, and rhythm are fashioned and blended, and how they are used to grant expression to feelings and ideas, one can understand this gift on a new level and the contribution it makes to the fullness of life. All the emotions of the human condition can be revealed to us through the aesthetic effects of great music, with its tension and release, its rise and fall, its growth and decay, its rejection and accord, its development and reaffirmation, its struggle and peace. These are some of the means through which music makes its revealment to the human spirit. Carl Halter has expanded on this concept, confirming that one must learn to understand music as being much more than just tone or rhythm, or the simple reflection of sorrow or joy. What music reveals to us is none less than life itself.

We find affirmation and rejection, unity and adversity, growth and decline in all of life.... The composer says implicitly: "Here is how the experiences of life sound.... After you have heard how they sound, you will understand them better and have for all of life a sympathy which you did not have before and which you cannot get in any other way."

Listen carefully to a recording of Beethoven's Ninth Symphony or to any of Bach's gigantic organ fugues, and within the music you will hear struggles which can only be described as titanic. The composer has set in motion gigantic forces of sound and time which clash and contend to a climax of fury. On listening to such music it becomes obvious to us that the composer did not manipulate these massive forces merely to show that they exist and that he had the skill and strength to control them. An attentive and expectant listener inevitably is convinced that the composer has grasped forces and meanings which relate to life. Indeed, such music convinces us that the grasp of music extends, however feebly, to the divine and the eternal. Such music gives us an apprehension of ultimate reality, ultimate values, and ultimate destiny.[1]

These are some of the compelling reasons we are called to seek an ever greater understanding and appreciation of the special gifts this unique art has to offer.

Music and Worship

Because, as has been noted, the musical art can both *express* and *reveal* spiritual truths, music has, down through all history, been closely teamed with religion, the ultimate expression of the yearnings of the human spirit. Both music and religion address not the tangible, but the spiritual side of human beings. There may be no practical purpose for beauty, nor, for that matter, for faith. But whenever humankind has felt the need to communicate the most sacred expressions of the soul, some sort of music has been created. From primitive civilizations to the present, this unique art has risen to its highest purpose at such times. In Old Testament times, music was expected to assist in bringing about a spiritual experience with Divinity. Second Kings 3:14–16 (NRSV) records:

Elisha said, ..."But get me a musician." And then, while the musician was playing, the power of the Lord came on him. And he said, "Thus says the Lord,..."

Scholars, musicians, and clergy appear to agree on the close and historic association between religion and music. Consider the expressions in the following paragraphs:

> It would be difficult to name a human society, whether primitive or civilized, which has not used music in its religious ritual. In fact, in most early cultures music was predominantly religious in its significance. This is true of the simpler cultures of Africa and Polynesia as well as of the highly cultured Greeks.[2]
>
> Through more than 3,000 years of Hebrew and Christian history, music has been associated with worship, and the Bible contains much of our first heritage of worship song.[3]
>
> After the Word of God, only music deserves to be praised as the mistress and governess of the emotions of the human heart.... It is out of consideration for this power of music that the Fathers and Prophets willed, and not in vain, that nothing be more closely bound up with the Word of God than music.[4] (Martin Luther, 1538)
>
> Music's chief value for worship lies in the realm of the spirit. Music has the power to move the soul of man [sic] for good or ill. When music is used in the praise of God and for the edification of man, it has the power to lift man's soul to greater appreciation of God and His love for man.[5]
>
> The links between music and worship are deep-seated, for they both spring from a God-implanted desire to search for truth and order. Music is a manifestation of that search in the mental and physical realms, worship is its expression in the cosmic. What is more, God has ordered his creation in such a way that the unfolding of its truths is profoundly satisfying.[6]

Lovelace and Rice discuss four characteristics that give music such a close relationship to worship. The first similarity is the element of mystery that surrounds both beauty and religion. Neither can be easily explained or defined, they point out. The second similarity is that both music and religion are "inextricably intertwined with emotions." The third has to do with the creativity involved in both. "Worship is a creative encounter of man [sic] with God.... Music, like worship, must be created over and over." The final correlation noted by the authors is music's affinity to language. The use of music "heightens the emotional impact of words.... Music tends to appeal more quickly to the emotions while speech is designed to appeal more immediately to the intellect."[7]

Wunderlich comments further and quotes a passage of scripture affirming the last point made by Lovelace and Rice, the ability of the arts to help achieve the right balance between emotion and intellect in worship:

> The arts in the service of the Gospel reach us on the level of our intellect by disclosing the underlying meaning of the Gospel message. They reach us on the level of the emotions by stirring us inwardly and guiding our inner response to the message. Intellect and emotions. . . —both these dimensions of human life are essential in our worship and in our use of art as vehicles of worship. "I will pray with the spirit and I will pray with the mind also; I will sing with the spirit and I will sing with the mind also" (I Corinthians 14:15).[8]

It is vital to the long-range success of our worship encounters with Divinity that the whole person be engaged, both heart and head, both intellect and emotion. Content without passion can be lifeless, while emotion without substance can be shallow. Neither passion nor substance alone is enough, but it is the proper nurture and balance of both that is important to the development of whole persons.

The Arts and Human Life

The highest calling of the arts is to bring meaning and beauty to human life. One of the most significant capacities with which humans have been endowed is the ability to appreciate beauty. If we are truly created in the image of the Creator, this must also be one of the characteristics of God. If this were not so, what would be the reason for the unending display of beauty in both the grandest and most minute specimens of nature? And surely the creative instinct of the human being echoes in a small way the same characteristic of its Creator. Hustad maintains that the "God-given instinct for creating and enjoying beauty is universal" and that anthropology supports the Genesis implication of humankind being created in God's image by "showing us that all persons are aesthetic beings."[9] He continues:

> The cave dwellers of prehistoric Europe may not have had a written language, but they left drawings and paintings of rare beauty. Even in this 20th century, near-naked Auca Indians in Ecuador, who did not hesitate to murder threatening neighbors and witnessing foreign missionaries, enjoyed a distinctive folksong. The clothing, tools, and weapons of aboriginal peoples are invariably decorated with design and color. Tribe members often extend their artistry to their own bodies, carving lines with sharp rocks or rudimentary knives.[10]

There are arts beyond that of words with which music has historically been teamed. Remember that the realm of pure music is not that of description or representation. Its strength is the power to create an ambience, mood, atmosphere, attitude, or frame of mind. It can also compel people toward physical movement; it can make them want to move, march, or dance. Dance as expressive movement is an art form that has been particularly closely associated with music. This natural art is found in every culture as the expression of pure joy in entertainment and celebration. The rhythmic element of music addresses our kinesthetic sense, and we want to respond with movement. It can instill pride, joy, longing, or even sensual excitement.

An important part of the effect of the song "The White Cliffs of Dover" had to do with associations of sacrifice, conflict, pride, and patriotism from the war years in England. Music, more than any other art, seems to have the power to bring back memories and associations. That is why couples celebrating a romantic anniversary want to hear "their song." It is why music that is associated with key life events has such a strong effect on the emotions, at those times and for years to come.

What, then, is music about?

Music can be summarily described as expression through the world of sound. What makes music so appealing and effective? Nobody really knows, but we do know that music can be appreciated on several levels: the level of basic physical response (the "gut" level), the level of mood creation, the level of emotional expression and reception, and the level of intellectual appreciation and understanding. All of these can be experienced simultaneously. Most of them come naturally to us, except the last. But when our natural, instinctive response to music is complemented by understanding, a new sense of fulfillment results and we begin to find more of the "fullness of life" available to us.

We soon discover that this special art demands no less than our best. It calls us to make intelligent and informed choices, and to commit ourselves to a program of continued growth in understanding and ability. Our acceptable offerings and our fulfilling enjoyment of this art will not come from the leftovers of our lives, but rather from the choicest of our "first fruits," the very best that is within us.

Part of the purpose of Part II is to help the reader understand how to listen to and participate in music more intelligently and meaningfully. Just what should one listen for in music? In answering this question, several of the most important elements or building blocks of music will be mentioned. The main elements of music are usually thought of as:

Melody—the tune, the main "theme"; several tones heard in succession.

Rhythm—the way music moves; the pattern and organization of the pulse or beat.

Harmony—the foundations of music; chords (several tones heard simultaneously).

Form—the way music is organized; patterns of musical phrases, sections, and movements.

In Part II, hymn tunes of several styles and eras will be used to illustrate "what makes music tick." For additional depth and further listening pleasure, references will also be made to music masterpieces that illustrate the points under discussion. Through exploring these examples of beauty, we can learn to appreciate and better understand what we might otherwise take for granted, and we can open new doors of awareness that will enrich our lives.

Notes

1. Carl Halter, *God and Man in Music* (St. Louis, Missouri: Concordia Publishing House, 1963), 36–37.
2. Robert E. Wunderlich, *Worship and the Arts* (St. Louis, Missouri: Concordia Publishing House, 1966), 93.
3. Donald P. Hustad, *Jubilate II* (Carol Stream, Illinois: Hope Publishing Company, 1993), 129.
4. Quoted in Halter, 10.
5. Carl Halter, *The Practice of Sacred Music* (St. Louis, Missouri: Concordia Publishing House, 1955), 9–10.
6. Andrew Wilson-Dickson, *The Story of Christian Music* (Oxford: Lion Publishing, 1992), 11.
7. Austin C. Lovelace and William C. Rice, *Music and Worship in the Church* (Nashville, Tennessee: Abingdon Press, 1992), 15–19.
8. Wunderlich, 47.
9. Hustad, 4.
10. Ibid.

PART TWO

Music and Our Hymns

Who sing, must seek to understand.
—Vida Smith, "One Day
When Fell the Spirit's Whisper"

Part I was focused on the importance of music in the worship experience. All too often worship is approached as a matter of routine, without taking full advantage of what could be experienced with a greater sense of awareness. How can one learn to better appreciate the gift of music, in daily living as well as in moments of worship?

The premise of Part II is that there are easily discovered concepts and relationships that will enable us to sing and also listen to music with greater understanding and appreciation. A good place to begin is by taking a closer look at the music of the hymns we sing so often. As we consider hymn tunes in different styles and from different eras, we can learn something about how music works, and also how the musical expression of a certain age is related to the underlying spirit of that time. Our goal is to gain a better appreciation of this unique gift in order to enrich our lives—to participate more completely in the eternal quest for the fullness of life, created for us and freely offered to us for the taking.

The tunes to which we sing hymns have been written in a number of styles and by a variety of people over many years. Most of these people were not famous. Sometimes their tunes were original, and sometimes their melodies were adapted from other sources, such as folk songs, popular songs, or the chants of the early Christian church. There are a number of hymn tunes in common use today, however, that have come from the pens of famous composers. Most of these tunes were not originally written for hymns, but have been adapted by other people from the concert music of these masters. Nevertheless, it is primarily the music of these masters that will be examined on this journey of musical discovery.

The order of the hymns discussed in Part II will be chronological in time rather than according to their numerical order in the hymnal. In order to better see relationships and the results of change through time, we will begin with early music and progress to the present day. As anyone who owns a "classic" automobile or a Stradivarius violin well knows, advanced age does not necessarily equate with less value. Quite the opposite is often true. In fact, creations having a beauty of design or inherent timeless quality will grow in value as the years progress. Similarly, music masterpieces that have stood the test of time and demonstrated their quality through the years are at least as satisfying today as are the latest tunes, some of which will be forgotten tomorrow.

While most of the hymns cited here can be found in a number of current hymnals, we will use *Hymns of the Saints* as our major resource. A hymn number, whether or not it is preceded by the abbreviation, "*HS*," indicates the number of the hymn in that hymnal. Both this chapter and the next should be read with hymnal in hand to better appreciate the discussion of each hymn.

Music from the Middle Ages (450–1450)

220   Of the Father's Love Begotten
music from Gregorian chant

We begin by looking at a hymn tune that has come down to us through several centuries, from the days of the high Gothic cathedrals and the beautiful (and instructive) stained-glass windows. Look only at the melody of this hymn, not the harmony which was added later. This thirteenth-century melody originated as Gregorian chant, the liturgical "plainsong" of the Middle Ages. It has a haunting, relaxing quality about it. It possesses simple grace and elegance, an elemental beauty and serenity that speak to a need felt by many in today's complex world. In fact, the world of commercial music has recently "discovered" the liturgical chant of the Middle Ages, as recordings by monks and other groups have become popular.

The chant of the Middle Ages is a perfect example of what is called **monophonic** (literally, "one-voiced") music, that is, music limited to only a single melodic line. All music up until about a thousand years ago was monophonic in texture. When the Bible relates that Jesus and the disciples sang a hymn, one might immediately think of the stirring strains of "Redeemer of Israel," with its strong, four-part harmony, perhaps accompanied by a large organ. Actually, the music Jesus knew would be more similar to the melody of this thirteenth-century plainsong, a type of music that has been preserved and can still be heard today in Jewish synagogues or Roman Catholic monasteries.

The melody of *HS* 220 was meant to be sung freely, letting the music flow with the natural rhythm of the words. It can have something of an undulating quality, a natural rise and fall as the phrases expand and then resolve to the breathing points. (Incidentally, it should be noticed that the text of this hymn has come down to us all the way from the fourth century.) Other examples of hymn tunes in *Hymns of the Saints* that originated with chant include *HS* 211 ("O Come, O Come, Emmanuel") and *HS* 283 ("Come, O Creator Spirit, Come").

Even though we can still enjoy the music of these worshipers of long ago, the monumental differences in our culture and our understanding of the world have given us a much different perspective and belief system. For many people, medieval life was so difficult and miserable that escape to a better world to come appeared to be the only answer. The faith of these people was centered in a rather remote God who sat in judgment on them as they tried to struggle through a torturous existence beset by devils and demons on every hand. They tended to personify the forces of good and evil and imaged a stern, grandfatherly personage who lived somewhere just above the clouds, surrounded by a winged entourage and immersed in constant battle with a horned, satanic figure who lived below the ground and kept forever aflame the white-hot fires of eternal punishment. Even though many churches today are deemphasizing the personification of evil (*Hymns of the Saints* contains only three references to the "devil" or the "tempter"), it may be obvious that these ways of thinking are by no means unknown in the late twentieth century, a time and culture far removed from the experience.

Music from the Renaissance (1450–1600)

255   Lo, How a Rose E'er Blooming
music arranged by Praetorius

Imagine sitting in a spacious cathedral looking at the awe-inspiring sights around and above you, and listening to magnificent music echoing throughout the sanctuary. Here is a hymn of Christmas that cries out for the sound of a choir lifting its voices to high Gothic arches and reverberating through a large European cathedral. The melody was harmonized by Michael Praetorius in the late Renaissance and shows the simple, pure harmonies that worshipers enjoyed then, and that still provide us today with a sense of peace and serenity. Note that there is no meter signature because the rhythmic pattern of this music changes freely from four beats per measure to six and back again. The composer's desire was to make the hymn flow naturally and vocally with the rhythm of the words rather than to mold the music to a consistent number of beats throughout.

In later musical periods the pattern of strict chordal style was the norm for hymn tunes, and it is still the most frequently used style in our own day. That is, four voice parts are written and tend to move together on each syllable or word. In this early hymn, however, note that one of the predominant features of Renaissance music—**polyphony**—is used briefly at the ends of several phrases. Whereas **monophony** is defined as music of only one voice, polyphony describes the use of several voices moving independently from one another; that is, the interweaving of equally important melodies, as in a round, for example. This technique, when used throughout a piece, gives the music a sense of motion and a flow that is beautiful to hear.

In this hymn, at the ends of each of the three main phrases, in measures 4, 8, and at the end, the four parts momentarily separate and move on their own, singing the words at slightly different times. This is only a small example of an important facet of Renaissance church music, so widely practiced that it began to be seen by church authorities as a problem. In many cases, too much musical creativity appeared to overshadow the clarity of the text, and church leaders began to object that the words could not be understood clearly.

The text of this famous German carol is taken from the poetic prophecy of Isaiah 11:1, "There shall come forth a rod out of the stem of Jesse, and a Branch shall grow out of his roots."

196 The Lord Our God Alone Is Strong
music by Thomas Tallis

Here is another hymn tune that illustrates the practice of polyphony even more clearly than *HS* 255. This tune, known as Tallis' Canon, was written by the prominent English Renaissance composer, Thomas Tallis. He was organist at the Chapel Royal and a famous composer of masses, magnificats, motets, anthems, and other English church music of the sixteenth century.

A **canon** (with one "n") can be compared to a simple "round," where one voice or group of voices begin a melody, and another voice or group comes in with the same melody a certain number of beats later. This is a simple illustration of the technique of polyphony, where the texture of the music is made up not of one melody alone (monophonic music), or even of a melody supported by a subservient accompaniment (homophonic music), but rather a blending of several melodies of equal importance and prominence. (In the case of a canon, what is blended together is actually the same melody appearing in different voices.)

HS 196 appears in *Hymns of the Saints* in two different forms. The first, on the left-hand page, is the traditional four-part harmonization. On the right-hand page is the actual canon, in which the same melody sung against itself produces pleasing harmony. Of course, most melodies would not sound **consonant** sung or played against themselves, but rather **dissonant** (tension producing). Melodies that are intended to be used as a canon or round, or even in the later, more sophisticated baroque **fugue**, have to be especially written for this purpose, a most challenging exercise for any composer.

Perhaps it is not stretching a point too much to discover a lesson in social dynamics through this music. Because a great deal of polyphonic music is written not for the same voice answering itself, but for two or more different melodies that harmonize when they come together, an interesting analogy comes to mind. When one speaks of a group of people working "in unison," what is literally meant is that they are all singing the same song. It would no doubt be preferable to encourage the idea of working "in harmony," or more accurately, "in polyphony." That would mean that everyone would be encouraged to sing their own unique and distinctive melodies, but that through the gifts of leadership, these different songs might be combined into a beautiful and rich multitextured fabric resulting in a satisfying and meaningful whole, significantly better than the sum of its parts.

Other important, and perhaps better known, examples of the use of polyphony, or **counterpoint**, in the hymnal would be those hymns containing a **descant**. A descant is another melody added *against* the main melody (thus a **countermelody**) and is intended to be sung by the higher voices on the last stanza of a hymn to give added interest and exitement and a sense of climax.

142 A Mighty Fortress Is Our God
text and music attributed to Martin Luther

The vision of the worth of the individual was a key concept in the new spirit of "humanism" that characterized the period of the Renaissance (literally "rebirth"). Inseparably bound up with this new era was the Reformation of the Christian church. This hymn by the chief reformer himself, Martin Luther, comes from that pivotal movement.

One of Luther's key concerns, closely related to the spirit of humanism, was that ordinary people should have not only more responsibility for their salvation but also the ability to read the scriptures themselves and participate fully in the worship experience. For years the priests had told people what the Bible said and how to interpret the doctrines and laws of the church. Of course, the scriptures were in Latin, which was not widely understood; in fact, many people could not even read and write their native tongue. Just as they listened to the Bible being read from the high pulpits, so they listened to the choir singing the songs of the church to them. Worship was being carried on in their behalf by professionals.

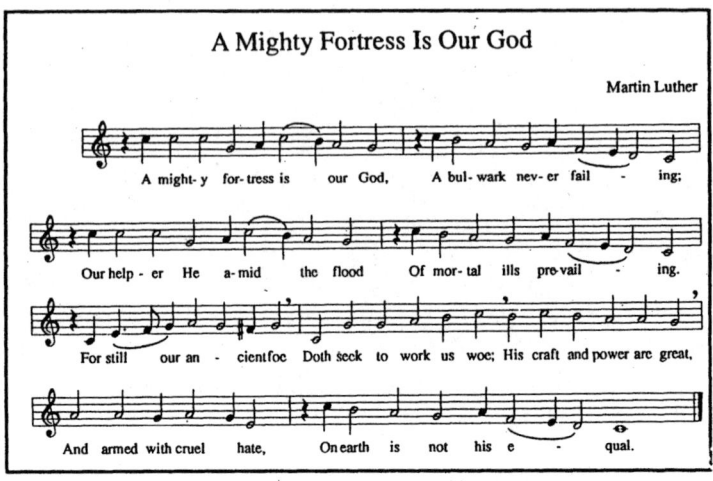

Luther moved to change all this. He wanted the Bible translated into German and read by everyone. He preached a new doctrine of inclusiveness which affirmed that the common person was just as important as the priests, the doctrine he called the "priesthood of all believers." And significant to our study here was his encouragement of full participation by the common person in the worship services of the church. Luther saw to it that new hymns were written that everyone, not just the choir, could sing. These hymns were in the people's own language and were set to simple tunes that could be easily learned and remembered. At first the congregations sang unaccompanied but were eventually joined by the organ, a practice we still enjoy today.

Some of the tunes of Luther's hymns were original, but often they were borrowed from melodies the people would already have known. These sources included portions of the chant from the Mass (which was continued as the accepted pattern of worship) and also a number of tunes borrowed from popular secular songs. This most famous Reformation hymn, "A Mighty Fortress," has been called the "battle hymn of the Reformation." Luther's text is an adaptation of Psalm 46, and the tune was either composed by Luther himself or possibly adapted from an existing song of the day. We know it best as it is printed in *HS* 142, in its straight, chordal form which no doubt made congregational singing easier, but it originally had a much more lively and syncopated rhythm to it (see opposite page). Some of its language has been revised in the version appearing in *Hymns of the Saints* (see Part III, page 91).

43   Praise God, from Whom All Blessings Flow
music attributed to Louis Bourgeois

This hymn tune is an example of music from the Calvinist Reformation tradition. In contrast to Luther, the reformer John Calvin was suspicious of the use of music in worship. One of his goals was to return to the simple worship practices of the early church, as he understood them. His motto was "Only God's word is worthy to be sung in God's praise," and thus he did not allow original hymns to be sung, but rather metrical versions of the psalms from the scriptures.

John Calvin is most frequently criticized for his actions restricting music in worship. Though he seemed to favor the use of music in home and school life, he was extremely fearful that its seductive and distracting charm would be harmful to pure, public worship. Consequently, he discarded the choir and its literature completely, and Calvinist iconoclasts removed the organs from the formerly Catholic churches. The first worship at Geneva had no singing at all, and Calvin complained about the resultant "cold tone" in the services. When he went to Strasbourg, he was attracted to the German psalm versions heard in the Bucer services, whereupon he set several psalms in metrical French to tunes of Mattheus Greiter and Woflgang Dachstein.[1]

In view of this orientation, it is not surprising that tunes from the hymnals of the Calvinist denominations are apt to be more simple, straightforward, and unadorned than other tunes. It is interesting to note that *The Hymnal* (Herald House, 1956), which preceded *Hymns of the Saints*, tended to favor a style of hymnody that was dignified and stately. Thus more hymns were included that originated with various Calvinist Psalters (collections of metrical psalms for singing) such as the *Geneva Psalter* and the *Scottish Psalter*. Several of these can be found in *Hymns of the Saints* as well, and perhaps the most notable example would be this hymn, often referred to as "The Doxology." The tune is called "The Old Hundredth," signifying that it was used with the text of Psalm 100 ("Make a joyful noise unto the Lord, all ye lands"), adapted to fit the meter of the tune. This metrical adaptation is still sung as the "Old Hundredth" in England: "All people that on earth do dwell, sing to the Lord with cheerful voice."

Music from the Baroque Period (1600–1750)

262   O Sacred Head, Now Wounded
harmonized by J. S. Bach

This is music from the Baroque period, which has often been called the "Golden Age" of Protestant church music. It was a great age for the organ in church music, including organ playing, organ composition, and organ building. It was a time of musical giants, culminating in the careers of the celebrated George Friedrich Handel and perhaps the most highly revered of all, the "musicians' musician," Johann Sebastian Bach. While both composers excelled at writing instrumental and vocal music for the concert hall, it is Bach who spent a major portion of his career as the musical servant of the church. His music is ample testimony to both his devotion and his genius.

Hymns of the Saints contains several hymn tunes harmonized by Bach. They are characteristic of the style of sincere, solid, and stately hymnody of his time. One of the most famous of these hymn tunes, called *chorales*, is *HS* 262, often referred to as the "Passion Chorale." As can be seen by this example, the chorales were imbued with a feeling of strength and solidity. These characteristics result from the straightforward, deliberate movement of the quarter-note rhythm, enhanced by a change of harmony on nearly every beat. In practice, there would have been a pause (notated today by a "bird's eye," or *fermata*, in some editions) at the end of each phrase of the text. These pauses would have aided the congregations in the large cathedrals to sing with greater unity.

The tunes of many of these chorales were not original, but often came from existing Gregorian chants, or even from popular songs. In this case, the melody is from a popular song by Hans Leo Hassler in the sixteenth century. The original tune, a lively one full of syncopation (see below), was used with the German text which translates, "My peace of mind is shattered by a tender maiden's charms." About 1600 the tune was used as a setting for the sacred words which translate, "My heart is filled with longing." In its transition to the church, the rhythm was straightened out for congregational singing, and it became one of the best known chorales, "O Sacred Head Now Wounded," the Passion Chorale. Bach made several arrangements, or harmonizations, of this chorale and used it in various creative ways in his larger works.

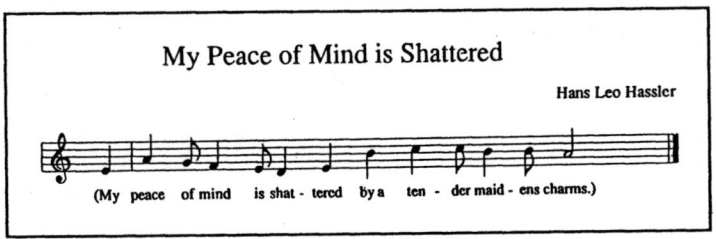

To appreciate what Bach could do with this same hymn tune, or chorale melody, listen to a recording of the last movement, the final chorus, from his *Christmas Oratorio*. Here Bach creates a festive atmosphere for the finale of this lengthy work for chorus and orchestra based on the birth of Christ. The orchestra, complete with joyful fanfares of trumpets in their highest register, sets a mood of triumph. This orchestral texture continues, and in due time the choir enters, not with an elaborate, complex challenge to the instruments, but instead with the most direct and meaningful contribution they could give—a simple hymn tune. As one listens to the several phrases of this hymn, punctuated by the continuing orchestral activity between each phrase, it becomes apparent that this is a hymn with a special meaning. It is none other than the Passion Chorale, the hymn listeners would have recognized as the very essence of the suffering and death of Christ, not his birth. But as the words to this setting of the chorale unfold, so does the testimony of J. S. Bach. For, as the great composer reminds us, it is only in the sacrifice of the Savior of humankind that the true meaning of his birth can be found: "...And mankind stands redeemed...before the Father's throne."

There are other chorale melodies with harmonizations by Bach in *Hymns of the Saints*. They include:

121 "Jesus, Priceless Treasure" (*Jesu, Meine Freude*). This tune by Johann Crüger was used with this same text by Johann Franck in Cruger's *Praxis Pietatis Melica* of 1653. Bach used the hymn in a motet and four cantatas, as well as several organ compositions. It is one of Bach's harmonizations that appears here.

227 "Word of God, Come Down on Earth." This contemporary hymn text is set to a tune named after the seventeenth-century text with which it was set, *Liebster Jesu, Wir Sind Hier* ("Blessed Jesus, We are Here"). J. S. Bach wrote a number of harmonizations of this tune for both organ and voice, including the one used in this hymnal.

498 "Forth in Thy Name, O Lord, We Go." This tune by the early seventeenth-century composer, Johann Schein, also has been given several harmonizations by J. S. Bach. The tune name, "Eisenach," is the name of the German village where Bach was born.

212 I Know That My Redeemer Lives
music by G. F. Handel

This is a hymn by the great Methodist hymn writer Charles Wesley, set to a melody by George Friedrich Handel, taken from his masterpiece, *Messiah*. It is the soprano solo, or *aria*, that opens Part III with an affirmation of the risen Christ. It will be obvious to anyone who has listened to *Messiah* that only a small part of the famous aria has been adapted for the purposes of this hymn tune.

Like Bach, Handel was a German organist and composer, but, unlike his contemporary, he achieved much more fame in his own time. Handel moved to London midway through his career, and it was there that he shifted his emphasis from opera to the closely related but religiously based form of oratorio, in his adopted language of English. He became a master at capturing the element of drama in his music. (For more about Handel and *Messiah*, see page 56.) Another of Handel's famous melodies from one of his other oratorios can be found as the tune for *HS* 395, "God of Creation" (see Part III).

Music from the Classical Period (1750–1820)

376 We Are Living, We Are Dwelling
music by F. J. Haydn

This hymn is set to a famous tune by one of the "fathers" of the Viennese Classical style of music, Franz Joseph Haydn. The simplicity and grace of the style period we call "Classical" followed as a natural reaction to the somewhat heavy, ornate style of the Baroque. Haydn was a key figure in the development of musical forms such as the symphony and string quartet. He also wrote operas and oratorios, including *The Creation*. The story of this particular tune, called "Austria," is related by Bradley:

> [This tune was written] for the Hapsburg emperor Francis II. The hymn was first performed on the emperor's birthday in 1797. It is said to have been a particular favorite of Haydn's and the story goes that it was the last piece of music that the composer ever played on his piano. It was first used as a hymn tune in England in 1805. Later it was taken up as the music for the German national anthem, "Deutschland! Deutschland! über alles" ["Germany over all"].[2]

One of the reasons this tune has become such a famous one is due to the fine craftsmanship it exhibits. This has to do with the clarity and balance of the phrase structure and the way the melody moves. It is important that music *go* somewhere, that there be a sense of movement to a climax and a resolution. **Climax points** are often the highest note in the melody, and when this height is combined with a bit of extra length the effect is a psychologically satisfying one.

Look at how those principles work in this tune. The first line of the hymn contains two well-balanced phrases, and the second line repeats them exactly. The third line is a contrast, taking the melody to its lowest point in the hymn. Then, within a few notes, the melody builds (supported by harmonies of anticipation) to a point where it can leap to its highest note in the beginning of the last line, enhanced by a bit of extra length as well. The tune is well fitted to this particular text, with the words, "Turn," and "Speak!" occurring on that grand climax. As with most well-crafted melodies, the tune comes to its final resting point, or **resolution**, soon after the climax has been reached. The musical and spiritual satisfaction of hymns can be enhanced when sung with understanding and awareness. One should sing *toward* these climaxes, and enjoy them when they are reached.

389 If Suddenly upon the Street
music by W. A. Mozart

This text has been set to a tune by the great genius of the Classical period, Wolfgang Amadeus Mozart. The tune was never intended to be a hymn tune, but has been "borrowed" from a famous duet (*"Bei Männern, welche Liebe fühlen"*) from Mozart's great opera, *The Magic Flute*. This hymn has been a popular one through the years, not only because of its graceful tune, but also the sentiments of its text.

Several features of the Classical style in music can be noted in the music of this hymn. Perhaps the most important is that it is the melody, the tune, that is the outstanding feature. During the Classical period, the common person became more interested in the arts, and composers tried to write music that was not so complex as many of the Baroque compositions. Classical period music tends to be less polyphonic and more homophonic, where there is a predominant melody rising above the accompanying harmony parts.

This hymn is probably most effectively sung in unison, because the harmony seems to be supplied simply in support of the tune. In the opera from which it came, the melody is sung by soloists above a somewhat subservient accompaniment from the orchestra. The phrase structure of the tune is clearly defined and well balanced. While that is true of most hymns, this balancing of melodic phrases is a notable feature of the Classical style. In fact, the musical phrases appear to follow a pattern of rise and fall, of question and answer.

Like Haydn's melody (*HS* 376 discussed above), this tune also shows the typical Classical pattern of repetition perfectly balanced by contrast. Note that, while the first phrase is repeated virtually without change in the third phrase, the phrases that follow the first and third are considerably different. In fact, it is the fourth phrase that begins the important contrasting section just before the end. Like all of

Mozart's music, the melody is a beautiful and graceful line, ideally suited for the human voice. Even the instrumental music of this composer sounds as if it could have been written for the voice. It has been said of Mozart, "All his music sings."

20 Joyful, Joyful We Adore Thee
music by Ludwig van Beethoven

The famous tune to this hymn is taken from one of the world's great masterpieces by one of the giants of Western music. The composer is Ludwig van Beethoven, and the masterpiece is his *Ninth Symphony*. Not only did Beethoven write music with an unprecedented degree of emotion and power, but he was a supreme innovator and an important transition figure for music. He began his career by composing music after the style of his contemporary Classical colleagues, but finished with music that was much more Romantic in spirit and style. Some critics call him a "Romantic Classicist," still others a "Classic Romanticist." But, as Donald J. Grout has put it, he is "neither Classic or Romantic; he is Beethoven, and his figure towers like a colossus astride the two centuries."[3]

This hymn tune is a good example of the use of simple "song form" in constructing a melody. This three-part form involves a first musical theme, a second contrasting theme, and a return to the first before closing. Entire symphony movements have been written using this structure, but as its name implies, it is frequently used in simple songs, including popular songs and hymns. (Because hymns usually contain four lines instead of three, the first theme is often repeated before going on to the second.) Keeping in mind that a musical theme can be a single melody, a small part of a melody, or a group of melodies, it is easy to see how this form can be adapted for pieces of varying length.

Look at the four lines (musicians call the lines "systems") in this hymn. It can be readily seen and heard that the melodic phrases in lines 1, 2, and 4 are nearly identical, with a contrasting melodic phrase occuring as line 3. If we were to call the first line "A" and the contrasting third line "B," we find that the four lines are organized in a pattern we could designate as AABA. Thus, the repetition of the main phrase serves to give the music unity, while the contrast of the third line gives diversity and a sense of climax and balance as the hymn goes on to finish with the main melody again. All great art has to have both unity and variety in order to provide both coherence and interest, and this simple "song form" fills the bill perfectly. Many hymn tunes follow this classic pattern of formal organization. For additional examples, look at *HS* 31, 32, 116, 136, and 182.

Music from the Romantic Period (1820–1900)

133 Cast Thy Burden upon the Lord
music by Felix Mendelssohn

This hymn has been adapted from one of the loveliest choruses from the popular oratorio, *Elijah*, by Felix Mendelssohn. Here was a German Romantic composer whose music was rooted firmly in Classical tradition. He composed symphonies, concertos, sonatas, and vocal songs in the old forms, but used the richer Romantic sounds.

Mendelssohn was influential in reviving interest in and general awareness of the music of J. S. Bach. He conducted the first performance of Bach's *St. Matthew Passion* since the Baroque composer's death. He greatly admired the works of both Bach and Handel, and his oratorio about the prophet Elijah was patterned after the dramatic Handelian masterpieces of the past. *Elijah* was composed in 1846 for the oratorio society in Birmingham, England, and therefore was sung in English. The premiere of the work is said to have been the high point of Mendelssohn's career. Sadly, Mendelssohn and Mozart were to share the dubious distinction of being child prodigies who composed prolifically but did not survive their thirties.

107 The Love of God, *and* 315 This Is My Song
music by Jean Sibelius

These hymns share a common melody from one of the best-loved compositions of orchestral music. It is a good example of the rich, flowing, lyrical melodic style composers of the Romantic period created. This was an era that emphasized freedom and emotional expression more than restraint and objectivity. It was also a time of great nationalism, which saw many countries of the world taking their place at the forefront of Western art and culture.

This famous tune was written in 1899 by the Finnish composer Jean Sibelius, as the main theme of his patriotic tone poem, *Finlandia*. The tune itself is not organized in the common AABA structure referred to with the discussion of *HS* 20. Instead, the six-line melody uses repetitions of three different melodic phrases, resulting in a form diagrammed as AABCBC. For a greater appreciation of this music, listen to the entire tone poem to discover the contrasting moods presented by the composer, climaxing in the unfolding of this beautiful melody.

Music from the Twentieth Century (1900–present)

375 The City Is Alive, O God
music by Gustav Holst

Here is another hymn tune that comes to us from a musical masterwork by a major composer. The tune is one of those in *Hymns of the Saints* that is not meant to be sung in harmony, but in unison. The music is taken from the suite, *The Planets*, by the English composer Gustav Holst. Like the theme of *Finlandia*, this sweeping melody is first heard following some contrasting introductory material. It serves as the musical centerpiece of the movment of the suite called "Jupiter, Bringer of Jollity." The suite was written in 1917 in the little village of Thaxted, after which the hymn tune is named. The five phrases of this melody can be diagrammed as AA^1BCA^1, where the superscript (^{1}) is used to designate a slight variation on the A theme.

480 For All the Saints
music by Ralph Vaughan Williams

This tune is a good example of the outstanding hymn tunes written in England during the present century. Ralph Vaughan Williams, a fine composer in his own right, was asked to head up the compilation process for the English hymnal of 1906. His hesitation to take on this task was overcome when he came to realize that, in those times, the music people heard in church was, for the most part, the only music in their lives. Therefore, he decided, it ought to be good music worthy of their singing and of their faith. To this end, Vaughan Williams selected the best hymn tunes available at that time, and when a good tune could not be found, he either rearranged an existing one or wrote a new one. To this day, some of the finest tunes we have are a result of his efforts.

It is impossible to hear this venerable tune without catching a glimpse of the majesty of the eternal Creator. The composer accomplished this breadth of feeling by the majestic sweep of his soaring melodic line and by the effective use of an opposing bass line. Vaughan Williams's hymns are models of this compositional technique of "contrary motion" between the top and bottom voices. As the melody ascends to a high point, the bass line moves inexorably downward, creating for this hymn a marvelous feeling of breadth and expansiveness which illuminates the concept of the God of the ages revealed in the text.

Vaughan Williams's love for English folk song also resulted in a number of beautifully flowing hymn tunes based on those sources. Examples of hymn tunes that stem from English folk song include the tunes "Kingsfold," used for *HS* 182 ("Make Room Within My Heart, O God"), and "Forest Green," used with both *HS* 370 ("Eternal God, Whose Power Upholds") and *HS* 484 ("Make Us, O God, a Church That Shares").

A contemporary Englishman who has written a great deal of religious music in a very accessible style is John Rutter. Listen to the pleasing, almost popular, sounds of his *Requiem*, in which the traditional Latin text of the Mass for the Dead is set to fresh new music.

155 Sometimes a Light Surprises
music by Jane Marshall

The contemporary church musician Jane Marshall has written a lively tune for this hymn which illuminates the ideas of "light" and "surprise" found in the text. This tune is a good illustration of rhythmic syncopation and changing meters in music. Often a piece of modern music will not stay in the same meter throughout, but will change from time to time, even perhaps with every measure. In this case, the rhythmic complexity results from a desire to give a fresh treatment to the text, with a more flexible and fluid pattern of accents. Interestingly enough, this also happened in very old music, such as Luther's original tune to "A Mighty Fortress" (see page 38), although in that case the meter signatures of each measure are not written in.

As has been noted, early music such as Gregorian chant also uses freely changing pulse patterns and is normally written without meter signatures, an effect not dissimilar to that of shifting meters. In Jane Marshall's hymn tune, the "surprises" of changing meter patterns add an interesting authenticity to the thoughts expressed in the texts. Compare this with a setting of the same text to a tune with a consistent meter in *HS* 154, no doubt included for more accessible congregational singing.

Syncopation. Like the effect of changing meters, an element of interest and excitement can be imparted to music by stressing beats or portions of a beat that are normally not accented. For example, instead of the normal pattern of 1̲ 2 3 4, the accents could shift to 1 2̲ 3 4̲, or even 1 &̲ 2 &̲ 3 &̲ 4 &̲, where the & describes a subdivision of the main beat. For example, in *HS* 155, the accents at the beginning would be: 4 &|1̲ & 2 &̲ 3 & 4 &|1̲ & 2 &̲ 3 & |. A sense of excitement is gained by jumping ahead of the normal beat 3 accent on the word "light." The same thing happens on every 4/4 measure throughout the hymn, and in the 2/4 measure near the end.

For an illustration of how a major composer uses these same modern rhythmic techniques in an extended composition, listen to a recording of Aaron Copland's *Billy the Kid Suite*.

301 O God, Our Source of Truth
music by Richard Dirksen

The music, "Vineyard Haven," to which this text has been set illustrates an important technique used in twentieth-century musical composition. In addition to the technique of freely changing rhythmic meters (cited with *HS* 155, above), modern composers also feel the freedom to change **tonality**, the musical key center, frequently. This shifting of the tonal center results in a feeling of ambiguity, and it is one of the most important of all the innovations in twentieth-century music. As you listen to this music, you can hear the effect of tonal shift, which is felt at the points where the extra flats and sharps (accidentals) appear, where the composer briefly visits keys other than the key in which the piece began.

The American composer Richard Wayne Dirksen wrote this tune in 1974 for the installation of a new bishop in Washington Cathedral. It is named after a town in Martha's Vineyard, Massachusetts.

189 O Love of God, How Strong and True
music by Calvin Hampton

Here is an example of another type of contemporary music found in *Hymns of the Saints*. In this hymnal, there are several tunes that stem from simple folk-style melodies, and this tune has something of that flavor, but in this piece the composer has invested an unusual amount of sophistication and interest. There are actually four things going on simultaneously: (1) the rhythmic bass part, almost in the character of the Baroque continuo ("walking bass"); (2) the accompaniment chords, consistently on the afterbeats; (3) the unison melody itself; and (4) a countermelody that echoes the main melody, first during the sustained note of the main melody, and the next time before the sustained note is reached. Like *HS* 301, this skillful composition also contains a shift in tonality, as can be seen by the plentiful accidentals after the first four bars. This is probably a case where a composition looks simpler than it actually is. The composer named the tune, "De Tar," after a fellow American organist.

In Closing

Part II has briefly sampled some of the music written by a number of important composers. Opening the door to this exploration have been hymn tunes that have come down to us from their works. Most of these are in the time-honored chordal style with its four parts: soprano, alto, tenor, and bass. There are examples of other types and styles of music in

Hymns of the Saints. For instance, one of the features of this hymnal that sets it apart from its predecessors is the inclusion of many tunes not in the traditional chordal style, but rather in melodic or folk-song style. While these can be sung in harmony, they are primarily intended to be sung in unison. Examples of this style include *HS* 22 ("Morning Has Broken"), *HS* 345 ("You Satisfy the Hungry Heart"), and *HS* 382 ("Freely, Freely").

It is interesting to note that a number of older gospel hymn tunes have also been included in *Hymns of the Saints*, some of them brought back from earlier hymnals and often matched with new words. Such tunes are usually marked by strong, sometimes march-like rhythm and simple, repetitive harmonies, frequently with repeated phrases or refrains. Examples of this style include *HS* 215 ("Tell Me the Story of Jesus"), *HS* 322 ("O How Blessed Are the Poor in Spirit"), and *HS* 48 ("Great and Marvelous").

Obviously, there is more to discover about music than can be learned simply from the style of music used in hymns. We will venture briefly into several related areas in the following pages.

Beyond the Hymnal

More about Music in the Renaissance

The Renaissance search for learning and discovery, freedom and individuality, expressed itself in the visual arts through clearly defined line and curving, smooth-flowing motion. The musical equivalent of these same predilections resulted in an emphasis on polyphony—music woven, or more precisely interwoven, out of several melodies and countermelodies, none of which is more important than the rest.

One of the best ways to catch a glimpse of the beauties of polyphonic music heard by worshipers during this era is to listen to the church music of the Italian composer Palestrina, referred to earlier. The music he wrote was of such loveliness and purity that the Catholic Church, during the Counter Reformation, used it as a model for other composers to follow. In his own time, Palestrina was called the "Prince of Music" because of his polyphony of great purity and technical perfection.

A good example of Palestrina's music is his *Pope Marcellus Mass*, written in 1563. It is dedicated to Pope Marcellus II, who was on the papal throne when Palestrina sang in the papal choir. It is written for six voice parts and is to be sung *a cappella* (literally "of the chapel"), in other words, without accompaniment. Kamien says of the *Kyrie* movement:

> Its six voice parts constantly imitate each other, yet blend beautifully.... The elegantly curved melodies summon the spirit of Gregorian chant. They flow smoothly and can be sung easily. Upward leaps are balanced at once by downward steps.... The text is short, and words are repeated with different melodic lines to express calm supplication. The rhythm flows continuously to the end of each section, when all voices come together on sustained chords.[4]

Another composer of the late Renaissance who wrote music of awe-inspiring magnificence was a fellow Italian, Giovanni Gabrieli. Much of his music for various combinations of organ, choirs, and instruments is **antiphonal** (answering) music, written to take advantage of the various galleries in the famous basilica of St. Mark's in Venice. This music might be called "the first great stereophonic sound," because Gabrieli loved to have the musicians echoing and answering one another from the two lofts, then blending together in great majesty. Listen to a recording of his music for antiphonal brass choirs, or for brasses and organ. What better way could the human spirit find to express the mystery of Divinity than in sounds so majestic and glorious?

More about Music of the Baroque

Bach. One of the chief reasons Johann Sebastian Bach is revered as one of history's great geniuses is his extraordinary skill in the art of **counterpoint** (a combining of several opposing or countering melodies meeting at numerous strategic points), another way of describing polyphonic music. He could look at a melody, or create one in his mind, and immediately think of numerous creative ways to use it in a complex fabric of imitation. His many fugues are good examples of skill at counterpoint which remains unequaled to this day. What is even more astounding is that he was able to *improvise* these complex pieces at the keyboard on the spot!

Listen to any of Bach's organ fugues and try to follow the first melody you hear as it is imitated by other voices and as it reappears throughout the composition accompanied by a variety of new material. It starts out like a campfire round, but immediately becomes more sophisticated and complex. Bach's fugues were usually preceded by a short introductory piece in the style of improvovasion. When a fugue is coupled with these pieces, titles such as Prelude and Fugue, Fantasia and Fugue, or Toccata and Fugue are the result.

Bach spent much of his life as a devoted church musician, and has left us many musical masterpieces based on religion. Among these are his **cantatas**, accompanied vocal or choral compositions, most of which were written for specific church services. Bach composed hundreds of these, but in his humble way did not consider them important enough to keep, with the result that many have been lost. He also wrote longer compositions for voices and instruments for the purposes of the concert hall. These have religious texts and are called **oratorios** and **Passions**. The Passions are settings of the biblical texts concerning the crucifixion of Jesus.

In many of his cantatas, as well as in his oratorios and Passions, Bach would insert at strategic points a well-known chorale (hymn), appropriate to the occasion, that the congregation would recognize. As noted earlier when discussing the Passion Chorale, the creative use of these hymn melodies can serve as a good introduction to the art of this master composer.

Oddly enough, in his own time, Bach was not widely known as a composer, but was better known as an organist. Another way he used the hymns of the church was in his organ preludes. Many of these were written down, and today we have them as examples of organ compositions that feature hymn melodies in a variety of interesting ways. Because of their musical interest and their noble character, these remain as one of the staples of the church organist's repertoire.

Handel. J. S. Bach was not the only great composer of the Baroque period, although he was certainly the finest composer of church music. George Friedrich Handel, while not a church musician, did compose some music for the church and, more importantly, he wrote a number of works with religious texts for the concert hall. A native of Germany, Handel culminated his career in London, England, drawn there because of his fame as a composer of Italian opera. Due to the changing tastes of his audiences, he began to write oratorios, similar to operas but without staging and acting and based on religious texts such as stories of biblical heroes.

Because Handel's oratorios were written in English, they have become well known to the English-speaking part of the world. Best known among them, of course, is *Messiah*. It is a well-known fact that Handel wrote this three-hour work in only twenty-four days, and that performances of it were first given for purposes of charity. More significant is the fact that its text is drawn from some of the most stirring passages from the Bible, selected by an Englishman named Charles Jennings.

Among Handel's oratorios, *Messiah* is unique in that it uses the New Testament as well as the Old, and does not have specific characters or a plot. Instead, the drama is supplied by the music itself, by the soloists, and by a chorus with a more expanded role than usual. This is the story of the life of Christ, told in three parts. Part I deals with the prophecy of the Messiah's coming, the announcements of his birth, and humankind's redemption through his coming. Part II has been described as "the accomplishment of redemption by the sacrifice of Jesus, mankind's rejection of God's offer and mankind's utter defeat when trying to oppose the power of the Almighty."[5] Part III is a climactic expression of faith in the victory of eternal life through the redemption of the Messiah.

This famous work can serve as an introduction to the several types of compositions that make up the forms we know as opera and oratorio. The forces for performing these works include an orchestra, chorus, and vocal soloists. *Messiah* begins, as do many large-scale Baroque compositions, with an orchestral *"ouverture"* in the French style. As is the convention for this form of overture, it starts with a slow section containing dotted (long-short) rhythms and progresses quickly to a fast section in the style of a fugue before ending with a final slow passage.

Two general types of vocal solos are found in an oratorio. The first is a **recitative**, which features the soloist singing with considerable rhythmic freedom, almost in the style of sung speech, accompanied only by strategically placed chords by the harpsichord and bass instruments (the "continuo"). The emphasis in a recitative is on telling or declaring something, and usually a significant amount of text is involved. The first solo for tenor in *Messiah*, "Comfort Ye, My People," is an example of a recitative. Recitatives are usually followed by a second type of solo, called by the Italian term **aria** ("air" or melody). A good example is the next piece, "Every Valley Shall Be Exalted." This is a full-fledged vocal solo in continuously flowing rhythm and with a distinctive melody, fully accompanied by the orchestra. Arias may comment on what has been declared in the recitative and often contain examples of the Baroque technique of "text painting." For example, Handel writes a long, soaring vocal "run" or **melisma** to paint the word "exalted." Similarly, he takes the tenor down low on the words "made low" and smooths out the melody on the words "the crooked straight." This was the expected convention in setting text in this period, and it is intriguing to look and listen for the many examples of text painting found throughout *Messiah*.

Much of the drama of *Messiah* is contained in the choruses, and is achieved by Handel through the frequent use of contrasting **dynamics** (volume) as well as contrasts between polyphonic and homophonic writing. Notice, for example, the drama depicted in the chorus, "For unto Us a Child Is Born." The sopranos are the first to announce the birth, then the tenors take over and spread the word, then both combine their efforts, and finally the news is spread to the other sections of the choir. When it is proclaimed that "the government shall be upon His shoulder," the music becomes imposing and important sounding through the use of dotted rhythms. To climax his message, Handel keeps things relatively restrained until the point where the chorus suddenly explodes into majestic block chords on the words naming Jesus as, "Wonderful, Counsellor, The Mighty God, The Everlasting Father, The Prince of Peace." This is an example of the dramatic effect achieved when the musical texture suddenly changes from polyphony to homophony. It is a rewarding experience to study this entire work, or any great work of music for that matter, in this kind of detail and hear the music with enlightened ears, on a deeper level of appreciation.

Baroque Instrumental Music

The film industry has recently "discovered" certain great composers and used some of their music as soundtrack material. This is particularly true of the instrumental music of another Baroque composer, Antonio Vivaldi. Listen to one of the many **concerti** (solos with orchestra) or one of the **concerti grossi** ("solos" for several players with orchestral accompaniment) by Vivaldi, Bach, or Handel. Vivaldi's *Four Seasons* or the *Brandenburg Concertos* of Bach would be good choices. These pieces are typically filled with high energy and a strong rhythmic drive. In them you can easily hear several key characteristics of Baroque music, including the prominent, continuous "walking bass line," called the **basso continuo.** You can also hear the Baroque concept of unity of mood throughout a movement, with the contrasts supplied by changes in instruments and dynamics.

More about Classical Form

To learn how **form** (musical organization) is employed in longer, full-fledged musical compositions, one needs to listen to an entire symphony and discover the form of each movement. In these instances, the use of form is seen in organizing not just short melodic phrases, as in hymns, but whole melodic sections which themselves make up a movement of a larger work. A good symphony with which to begin would be Mozart's Symphony in G minor, also called Symphony no. 40. Like most Classical symphonies, it has four movements. The third movement is a dance-like movement using the form and style of the Classical "minuet." The minuet and trio is a three-part form, with the minuet being the "A" and the trio the "B." Because the minuet is repeated after the contrasting trio, the overall form of the minuet and trio is a perfectly balanced ABA form.

Sonata form. The other three movements of Mozart's Symphony in G minor (movements 1, 2, 4) are all written in the same form, and provide a good illustration of the frequent use of one of the most dominant forms during the Classical period—"sonata form." It may also be called "sonata-allegro form," because it was used for nearly all first movements (marked *allegro*, or "fast") of instrumental sonatas, symphonies, and concertos. Sonata form also features opening material that is repeated again at the end of the movement after a contrasting central section, in other words, our familiar ABA structure. But the genius of this form lies not only in its balance and in the contrasts that occur within the overall A sections, but in the tremendous creativity encouraged by the middle B section, called the "development." Here, the composer may take one of the melodies or melodic phrases introduced up to that point and change its pitch, style, and mood, and elaborate on it and generally explore it—in other words, "develop" it.

Follow movements 1, 2, and 4 of Mozart's Symphony in G minor, using the following outline of sonata form. Notice that we call the first section of the larger ABA structure the **exposition**, and the last section the **recapitulation**. The middle section (the larger B) is the **development**. However, within the exposition and the recapitulation there are two contrasting themes, the A and B themes, with B usually being a softer or more lyrical contrast to the stronger A theme. These two primary themes are separated by transitional musical material which is normally not as important as the A and B, but which simply takes us from one to the other. These "filler" sections can be called the "bridge" and "closing" sections of the exposition and recapitulation.

Outline of Sonata-Allegro Form:
Exposition (larger A section)
    A theme
        bridge theme
    B theme
        closing theme
Development (larger B section)
    Segments of A or B or bridge themes
    Changes in pitch (key) and mood
Recapitulation (larger A section)
    A theme
        bridge theme

B theme
    closing theme

The concept of "development" is one of the great ideas in art music, and it is one of the key contributions of the Classical era. In the development, one of the melodies used at the beginning (usually the A theme) is subjected to examination and exploration under a variety of situations, much like getting better acquainted with a good friend. Then, when that theme returns in the recapitulation, how exciting and fulfilling it is to see (more accurately to hear) that old friend again, in the light of the intimate detail that has now been learned.

Rondo form. For a lighter moment in listening, choose a final movement of one of the concertos of Mozart or Beethoven, which normally use the rondo form. This form is like a "Dagwood" sandwich, with several contrasting sections appearing after repetitions of the main theme (the "bread"), usually a buoyant, dance-like tune. The diagram of this form would be: ABACADA.

More about Beethoven's Ninth Symphony

Listen to the last (fourth) movement of Beethoven's Symphony no. 9, which contains the theme used in *HS* 20 and also *HS* 470. One of Beethoven's most notable innovations was to add a chorus to the last movement of this symphony. As his contemporaries were quick to point out, a symphony is supposed to be a work for orchestra, not for orchestra and choir. But Beethoven wanted to affirm a message of worldwide community incorporating the words of Schiller's *Ode to Joy* into his masterpiece, so he added to the orchestra four vocal soloists and a choir.

After an orchestral introduction during which the themes of the previous three movements are heard briefly and rejected, Beethoven settles on his new theme for this movement. It begins quietly in the low strings; then a lyrical bassoon countermelody is added; and finally the theme is taken up by the rest of the orchestra. Suddenly the baritone stands and declares, "Friends, let us no more these sounds continue, let us sing." He then begins singing the hymn to joy, and is quickly followed by an enthusiastic choir. The entire movement contains a great deal of contrast as it portrays the various moods of the stanzas of the poem. At one point there is a little march as the text talks about "running the joyous race." Yet another notable section captures an ethereal mood as the choir testifies that "above the stars there dwells a loving Father."

This symphony was longer than any previous symphony, and composed for larger forces. Other innovations made by Beethoven in earlier symphonies include changing the normal order of the movements, going from one movement to another without a break, and generally taking new liberties with the traditional forms, expanding and altering them to suit his purposes. He even wrote a symphony with something of a descriptive nature (a "program")—his Symphony no. 6, the "Pastoral" symphony.

More about Romanticism

As we have surveyed the unfolding musical scene through several hundred years, an interesting and important feature may be noted. Over the years, there seems to be a pendulum swinging between two poles—the first a preference for order, tradition, and reason, and the second, a spirit of independence, emotion, and more personal expression. In the first, clarity of form, detail, and perfect balance are stressed; in the second, the emphasis is on freedom, subjectivity, exaltation, and fantasy. The first we call Classical, the second, Romantic. The music of both these eras offers an abundance of lyrical melody, but "Classical" music possesses an element of purity, delicacy, and grace, while "Romantic" music aims for more emotional richness, passion, and dramatic effects. Here we must hasten to add an important point and stress that there can be no art without feeling, and no art without form. The pendulum only marks the changing degree of emphasis on each of these factors.

A good introduction to the art music of the Romantic period would be the symphonies and overtures of Tchaikovsky. In them you can hear the unique flavor of their Russian roots, the richness of passionate melody and harmony, and the interest and color of constantly changing instrumental combinations and solos. Other important composers of this period include the pianist/composers Chopin and Liszt; the Austrian-Germanic composers Schubert, Schumann, Mendelssohn, and Brahms; the Italian opera composers such as Verdi and Rossini; the German music dramatist Richard Wagner; the Frenchmen Berlioz and Saint-Saëns; and many others from a variety of countries.

Toward the New Millenium

As the physical sciences advance toward new discoveries in the realms of time and space, as well as in the subminiature world of the atom, new worlds of exploration into being itself are being pursued through the avenues of biological science and psychology. Graphic artists and musicians alike have been influenced by the new perceptions of reality thus being opened up, and many of these artists are reflecting a new freedom to break from the most cherished conventions of the past. In the graphic arts of the past, the desire to express, exalt, and interpret some sort of reality had been the convention, while in music the tonal center traditionally served as its own anchor of reality. Now the spirit of a new age has brought with it the urge to experiment with new worlds of nonrepresentational art and **atonal music**. The reader is urged to pursue the almost limitless, ever changing lists of "isms" currently being espoused in today's artistic world.

One of the early movements in the direction of abstraction in visual art came at the turn of the century in France.

Called **impressionism**, the artist aimed not for a detailed representation of his subject, but rather for a somewhat vague impression of what the subject was like during a fleeting moment in time, in a given setting with certain lighting conditions, etc. Painters like Monet tried to capture the image quickly, using broad brush strokes, indistinct outlines, and colors tending toward the pastel end of the spectrum. The result of these techniques is normally a particularly pleasing and restful scene. Musicians, notably the Frenchman Debussy, endeavored to obtain a similar effect in music, using vague, indistinct tonality and exploiting the softer, more "pastel" sounds of harps, woodwinds, and shimmering, often muted strings.

Another diverse "ism" with a similar sounding name, but quite dissimilar goals, was the movement called **expressionism** in art and music. While not identical in both arts, it was an attempt to portray not a traditional image or a conventional musical idea but rather an expression of deep inner feelings, perhaps even tensions. In the graphic arts, this often resulted in deliberate and sometimes shocking distortions. In music, composers such as Schoenberg and his "disciples" achieved the complete absence of a key feeling (atonality) through techniques such as the **twelve-tone system**, which uses all twelve chromatic tones of the scale equally in various types of sequences. This technique can result in music of extreme dissonance.

Because we are still so close in time to the work of the twentieth-century composers, it is difficult to tell exactly which ones will emerge as the most important musicians of our time. There is one composer, however, whose place in history seems assured. He is the Russian-born Igor Stravinsky. This modern genius composed music in nearly all genres, and he did so with such imagination, innovation, musicality, and craftsmanship that his influence on the music of our century has been immense. Stravinsky came to prominence as a composer of music for the dance, such as his famous *Firebird Suite*, written for the Russian ballet. In 1910, his music for the ballet *The Rite of Spring*, about an ancient, primitive culture, was fittingly dissonant and primitive, so much so that it caused a riot at its premiere performance in Paris.

Also active early in this century were a number of composers who worked to compose fresh new music inspired by the indigenous melodies characteristic of their native lands. In America, Aaron Copland endeavored, quite successfully, to write music people would appreciate during his lifetime, rather than afterward. A similar orientation was shared by Bela Bartok in Hungary and Gustav Holst and Ralph Vaughan Williams in England. They all composed contemporary art music based on the folk songs and melodies of their own countries.

Notes

1. Donald P. Hustad, *Jubilate II* (Carol Stream, Illinois: Hope Publishing Co., 1993), 193.
2. Ian Bradley, *The Penguin Book of Hymns* (London: Penguin Books, 1990), 132.
3. Donald Jay Grout, *A History of Western Music*, 3rd ed. (New York: W. W. Norton, 1980), 521.
4. Roger Kamien, *Music: An Appreciation,* 4th ed. (New York: McGraw Hill, 1984), 112–113.
5. Ibid., 198.

PART THREE

Hymns of the Restoration

Since Love is Lord of heaven and earth,
How can I keep from singing?
—Robert Lowry, *HS* 157

Just what is a hymn? The easy answer would be to give a brief definition of this unique form of song. A hymn may be defined most simply as a song of praise or celebration. It is one of the most venerable of all musical forms. The ancient Greeks sang hymns to and about their many gods, as did the people of the Bible to and about their One God. In the present day, we have all no doubt sung hymns, but perhaps have not thought about what it is that makes this musical genre so singular and special.

Technically speaking, a hymn normally consists of several short verses of poetry set to music (the hymn tune) which is traditionally **strophic, syllabic,** and **congregational**. "Strophic" means that the music is repeated for each verse (or stanza) of the poem. "Syllabic" means that as a general rule there is roughly one melody note per syllable of text. And "congregational" means that the tune is a simple one suitable for singing by a congregation or individual worshiper, rather than by a special soloist or choir.

But hymns are much more than this. Perhaps a more complete understanding of these treasures can be discovered in their application. Through the years, hymns have been sung for a great variety of reasons. We sing hymns to learn more about Divinity. (How else did we all learn with such certainty that "Jesus loves me"?) We sing to discover thoughts and language more profound and beautiful than our own. We sing to express, within the fellowship of friends, our praise and adoration, our faith and trust, our devotion and commitment. We sing to share with others our joys and sorrows, our struggles and triumphs. We sing to cry out to our God, and in our song we hear his voice.

Latter Day Saints have always been a singing people. The history of this movement can be told in the hymns of the church. In his book, *Hymns in Worship*, Roger Revell discusses the various hymnals of the church's history, and a study of these would show the development of both musical and theological concepts among the Saints over the years. Some of these hymns are still sung today, while others have served their purpose and are no longer appropriate.

The present hymnal of the church, *Hymns of the Saints*, contains 501 hymns on a number of subjects and in a variety of styles. Many of them have become like old friends; others have yet to become widely known. The same could be said of the many authors and composers whose work is represented in our current hymnal. Every hymn, regardless of its age or the style of its text or music, has its own story and its own testimony, as does every author and composer. These are stories that need to be told and appreciated more widely. They are stories that can enrich the worship life of the church.

Numerous books are generally available that contain commentary on many of the world's best-known Christian hymns. However, a significant number of unique hymn texts, as well as hymn tunes, have been produced by members of the Reorganized Church of Jesus Christ of Latter Day Saints and included in *Hymns of the Saints*. They are surprising in both their quantity and quality. An attempt has been made in the pages that follow to provide commentary on many (but by no means all) of these fine hymns. It is hoped that this resource will prove helpful in using these hymns for the enhancement of both private and corporate worship.

In addition to comments on the hymns, information is given about the authors, and in many cases personal observations about the hymns by the authors themselves are included. I am grateful to the many living hymn writers represented here for their willingness to supply information about themselves and the hymns they have written. Although emphasis has been given to hymns that are new to *Hymns of the Saints*, a number of hymns have also been included that have played a significant part in the worship of the church for many generations. In preparing comments on those timeless expressions, I am indebted to the excellent information provided by Roy Cheville in his book, *They Sang of the Restoration* (1955), and by Carlyle Kueffer and others in the 1938 publication, *Stories of Our Hymns*, Herald House publications that are no longer in print.

This chapter, like the last, will be best read with the hymnal nearby. For ease of reference, the commentaries in this chapter are arranged in the order in which the hymns appear in *Hymns of the Saints*. Each is headed by its hymn number, the first line of text, the name of the RLDS author of the text, and the composer of the tune in those cases where there is an RLDS composer. The premise of this writing has been that greater knowledge and understanding results in appreciation on a deeper level. We are blessed with a remarkable history of hymnody in the Reorganized Church of Jesus Christ of Latter Day Saints. It is hoped that the comments and testimonies that follow will enhance the messages of these hymns and enrich the worship of all who sing them.

1 O Lord, Grace Our Communion
text by Geoffrey F. Spencer

Geoffrey Spencer spent the first thirty-eight years of his life in Australia, including his first twelve years as a World Church appointee. His parents encouraged the love he developed for music and singing, and the congregations he attended during those years gave him the opportunity to participate in choral music, both as a singer and sometimes as a conductor. Brother Spencer recalls one of the first special services for which he wrote some words and music to be included in the choir's presentation. The result was, he says, "no doubt amateurish, and long forgotten, but significant in that it was one more way in which I felt linked with the fellowship of the church."

As a high school teacher of English, "and occasionally a director of school choirs when the school was not large enough to merit a music specialist," Brother Spencer was able to indulge his love of the "word," both written and sung. "I was in those early years, and am still, remarkably susceptible to language, and deeply responsive to its persuasive powers, whether written, spoken or sung," he adds. Thoughout his life, Geoffrey Spencer has served the church through many offices and avenues of service, culminating in ten years as a member of the Council of Twelve, four of these as its president. He has said that during these years, the part of his work he most enjoyed was visiting in the many congregations around the church and participating in their worship.

As a result of his appointment to the committee that compiled *Hymns of the Saints*, Geoffrey Spencer saw clearly the need of the church for fresh new hymns on a variety of topics. He responded to this challenge by authoring or coauthoring no less than thirteen hymn texts for this hymnal. Among these can be found some of the finest and best-loved new hymns in the collection.

Brother Spencer has commented on the way the hymn-writing process works best for him:

My general method in developing a hymn text is strongly "perspirational." Rarely do I find lines coming easily and spontaneously. Most often I begin with a single notion, or germ idea, and let it rattle around in my mind. Phrases and terms tend to come at various intervals until I have the skeleton of a text. What follows after that is essentially hard work, dealing with rhyme, meter, freshness of language, and imagery.

"O Lord, Grace Our Communion" was chosen to be the first hymn in the new hymnal, in the category of "Gathering for Worship." The text is set to the Swedish folk tune called "Holy Wings." As is the case with all good hymns, it speaks those sentiments that should be ours collectively as we approach any worship experience, and it does so more beautifully than each of us might express individually.

2 Met in Thy Sacred Name, O Lord
text by Mark H. Forscutt

The author of this hymn was a dominant figure in the early Reorganization. His contribution was felt in many ways, but particularly through his leadership in the area of music. His legacy includes both hymn texts (see also *HS* 112) and hymn tunes (see *HS* 24, 151, and 436) that are still sung today.

Mark Hill Forscutt was born in Bath, England, in 1834. It was there that he came in contact with Latter Day Saint missionaries and was baptized at the age of nineteen despite strong opposition from his family. He and his new bride sailed for America on their wedding day, March 25, 1860, and traveled on foot from Omaha, Nebraska, to Salt Lake City, where he became the private secretary to Brigham Young. He soon became disillusioned with the Utah church. In those days, it was risky for "apostates" to leave the church, but by exchanging a stagecoach ticket with a soldier, he was able to escape safely without identification. He came into contact with the Reorganization and joined the young movement on New Year's Day, 1865.

Forscutt developed a close friendship with Joseph Smith III. His contribution to the Reorganization included his role as assistant editor of the *Saints' Herald* and editor of the church's first hymnal to contain music, the *Saints' Harmony*. He has been called "the most able and influential musician of the church" during this time. In this hymn, he has given us an earnest prayer of gathering which has been well sung by the church through the years. The tune, "Manoah" (the name of Sampson's father), has been arranged from a melody attributed to the nineteenth-century Italian opera composer, Gioacchino Rossini.

6 Lord, Thou Hast Brought Us to This Place
text by Dennis Aldridge

Dennis Aldridge was born in Yorkshire, England. After his secondary education, he chose to enter government service directly, spurning a place at university. He rose in the ranks of the Inland Revenue Service to become the regional controller responsible for the Service first in East London, then for the whole of Wales, and lastly for the southwest of the British Isles. When he retired from public service in 1993, Dennis Aldridge received the high honor of being appointed Commander of the Order of the British Empire by Her Majesty Queen Elizabeth II at Buckingham Palace.

Brother Aldridge has served the church through a variety of priesthood offices. His responsibilities have included those of pastor, district president, counselor to regional presidents, presiding bishop's representative, and chairman of Camp Quality UK (a camp for children with cancer), a position of service he still holds. As an evangelist, he frequently travels from his home in Devon to give ministry throughout the British Isles. Writing verse, principally to be used in hymns, is one of the ways he finds relaxation and enjoyment.

This hymn was written for the dedication service for Dunfield House, the British Isles church's conference center located in an area of great natural beauty near the border between England and Wales. Although Brother Aldridge had been intimately involved in the purchase and remodeling of this facility, he continued to be concerned about the investment needed to complete the task, and even began to believe that a mistake had been made in purchasing the house. One day in 1965, during a worship service at a work weekend at the facility, a brother stood to bear his testimony. Dennis remembers, "As he did so, I was bathed in the Spirit and felt the Lord asking me why I doubted, when he himself had chosen this place for us. From that moment, I ceased to doubt."

Dennis remembered that experience in 1980 when he was asked to write a hymn for the dedication service of the facility. He recalls,

> I began, believing that I knew what the first line would be: "Lord, Thou didst choose for us this place!" Having decided, as I believed, upon the first line, I wanted a strong tune that could help affirm faith and one which would be known to those attending the dedication service, whether they were regular church-goers or not. I had to make a train journey from Devon to London and decided to take my hymn-book along with me in order to find a suitable tune. "Melita" was the only tune in the church's hymnal of the day that would fit the bill, and would allow my chosen first line.
>
> I began to work in the train. I wanted the first verse of the hymn to emphasize—beyond the simple statement in the first line—that God had directed us to Dunfield House. As I sought ideas and rhymes, I was drawn to God's guidance of the children of Israel, "his chosen race," and I was made aware that we, too, were "a chosen people." The first line had to change to fit the ideas now flowing in. We had been *brought* to Dunfield House! I finished the first verse on the train, much to the interest of my fellow-passengers. A discussion about the church, and the house, ensued until we got to London! The remainder of the hymn was written in my hotel room. Verse two catches something of the wonder of my testimony of 1965 that God did choose the place for us, and my acknowledgement of the many blessings which have been ours in it. Verse three seeks to acknowledge the beauty that surrounds Dunfield as a wonderful gift from God. Verse four faces the dilemma of the question as to how we respond. What can we give to One who has given us so much—even when our faith acknowledges his goodness? With his help we can respond through our witness.

Although written for a specific occasion, this hymn has found a more universal place of honor in the hearts of many.

It is frequently used to express heartfelt appreciation for God's goodness as his people gather in worship, or as they begin adventures with him in new places. The tune, "Melita," by John B. Dykes, was written for the hymn, "Eternal Father, Strong to Save," first published in the English hymnal, *Hymns Ancient and Modern*, in 1861. That hymn, frequently sung in England, is a petition for the safety of "those in peril on the sea." It is known in the United States as the Navy Hymn. The name of the tune is the Roman name for the isle of Malta, where Paul was shipwrecked.

7 O Lord, Around Thine Altar Now
text by Charles Derry

This familiar gathering hymn was written in 1861 by Charles Derry, a native of Staffordshire, England, who had come to America as a member of the Utah church. He and his wife made the seven-week voyage from Liverpool to New Orleans in 1854. After making their way to Westport, near the present Kansas City, Missouri, they started out in a caravan of thirty-six wagons for Salt Lake Valley. His wife, Ann, died enroute, and Charles arrived in Utah with his two small children, now motherless. He remarried not long after his arrival, but soon became disillusioned with life in Salt Lake City. In 1859, the family left Utah and settled in Fontanelle, Nebraska, the home of Charles's brother.

Both his health and faith had been weakened by his experience in Utah, but Charles and his family were to have an experience in Fontanelle that he later credited with reviving his faith and providing the stimulus to write this hymn. One night a terrible storm arose, with high winds and fearful thunder and lightning. Before long, the lightning had started a fire in the dry grass in the valley, and the winds were blowing the fire toward the Derry cottage. Charles and his family were close to abandoning their home when his small daughter cried out, "O Father! I hope the Lord will bless us." Soon the wind changed and the family was saved. Not long after this experience, Charles came in contact with the Reorganization as a result of the efforts of W. W. Blair and E. C. Briggs, who had been working in western Iowa. After reading a copy of the *True Latter Day Saints' Herald*, he walked for miles through deep snow to meet the two men and was baptized in March 1861.

Charles Derry was ordained a seventy later that year and in December 1862, he was sent out on a mission to his native England. He became a leader in the Reorganized church, serving as a member of the Council of Twelve from 1865 to 1870, and as president of the high priests quorum from 1874–1901.

This hymn is sung to a tune written in London, England, in 1762 by Thomas Arne. Arne is famous for many popular English songs, including the music to "Rule, Britannia." Another frequently used hymn of praise from the pen of Charles Derry is "Lord, May Our Hearts Be Tuned to Sing" (see *HS* 26).

8 You May Sing of the Beauty
text by David H. Smith
tune by Norman W. Smith

The "Sweet Singer of Latter Day Israel," David Hyrum Smith, was born in Nauvoo, Illinois, in 1844, nearly five months after the assassination of his father, Joseph Smith Jr. He was a sensitive young man with interests in poetry, music, and painting, and with a love of nature expressed in this hymn. He used to spend hours at a special place of natural beauty near Nauvoo, a secluded wooded spot with a waterfall, known today as "David's Chamber." His young life was lived out under the strains of the struggling little group of church members who remained in Nauvoo and who had to be guarded in speaking about their faith in the light of strong opposition all around. He spent several years in the loneliness of the missionary field, including a mission to Utah. He was called to the First Presidency in 1873, and released in 1883. Mental illness ended the effective ministry of this highly gifted young man who had been born into one of the most stressful times in church history. He is the author of numerous hymns which are a treasured part of the heritage of the movement.

The authorship of the tune, "Fellowship," is uncertain, but it has been ascribed to Norman Whitefield Smith, who also composed two tunes for hymns by David's older brother, the prophet Joseph III. Born in Ohio in 1833 and baptized in Michigan in 1869, Norman Smith found ample opportunity to minister to the members of the young Reorganization through his music. The family moved to Lamoni, Iowa, in 1882 to join the new church community there. He was one of the four people who compiled the *Saints' Harp*, and he assisted in the work on the *Saints' Harmony*.

24 Blest Be Thou, O God of Israel
tune by Mark H. Forscutt

Here is a case where the hymn tune, not the text, was written by a member of the Reorganization. The story of Mark Forscutt's life has been told with *HS* 2, for which he wrote the words. An important church leader, Forscutt was also a self-educated musician. This tune, which he wrote for "Blest Be Thou," is one of the finest and best-loved tunes in the hymnal, and the circumstances of its creation deserve to be widely known.

Roy Cheville has related the composer's remarkable testimony of the writing of this hymn tune.

In one of Mark Forscutt's pastorates he spent considerable time in a room adjoining the church. One evening he sat reading alone. He became aware of organ music. He listened to the beautiful harmony. He presumed that the sister in whose home he was staying might be playing the home organ. She assured him she had not been at the instrument. Again he heard the strains of an organ. This time he went over to the church, thinking someone was playing the church organ. The church was empty and dark. He wrote down the melody he had heard and the harmony he recalled. Mark Forscutt, with his sensitivity to beautiful sound, was inspired through auditory inspiration. The celestial music he heard has lifted thousands of us heavenward.

The text of this beautiful hymn was written earlier in the nineteenth century by the rector of a church in New York City, Henry Onderdonk. It is a poetic paraphrase of the last prayer of King David recorded in I Chronicles 29:10–13. A reading of that scripture reveals how close the hymn's language is to David's prayer, offered in praise to the Lord for the congregation's generous giving to the building of the temple in that day.

26 Lord, May Our Hearts Be Tuned to Sing
text by Charles Derry
tune by Mary A. Bradford

Here is a hymn of praise and sincere devotion from the pen of one of the pioneers of the early Reorganization. Its language is consistent with the imagery of its time, but the praise it expresses is clearly that of both heart and hand. It is not just the celebration of emotion alone, but of the desire to get down to work with renewed dedication. The text may well have been based on Doctrine and Covenants 59:2.

> ...thou shalt go to the house of prayer and offer up thy sacraments upon my holy day; ...nevertheless thy vows shall be offered up in righteousness on all days, and at all times; but remember that on this, the Lord's day, thou shalt offer thine oblations, and thy sacraments, unto the Most High.

The author of the text was Charles Derry, a native of England, who was converted from the Utah church after becoming disillusioned with life in the Salt Lake Valley. His fascinating story is told with *HS* 7. *Stories of our Hymns* gives us additional detail concerning the mission of Charles Derry to his native England. We are told that during that mission,

> ...he carried the gospel to his mother who at that time told him she had dedicated him to the service of God when he was three weeks old. He baptized the first person uniting with the Reorganization in England. He was alone in the mission for some months and was hungry for news from home. Having no money, he pawned his overcoat to get from the post office four *Heralds* on which postage was due.... He labored in various parts of Great Britain, persevering in the face of discouragement.

The tune, "Gratefulness," was written by Mary A. Bradford, who was born in 1821 at Pawtucket, Rhode Island, and later made her home in Providence. It was there that she was converted to the church. She was a teacher of both vocal and instrumental music and served for many years as an organist for the Providence congregation.

33 The Spirit of God Like a Fire Is Burning
text by W. W. Phelps

This hymn grew out of the experiences surrounding the dedication of the Kirtland Temple in 1836. There remains to this day no other hymn that is sung by Latter Day Saints with more enthusiasm and excitement. The story of its creation is a unique one. W. W. Phelps (see *HS* 313 for more information) was with Joseph Smith and other church leaders in the important meetings that took place during the weeks leading up to the temple dedication. The Holy Spirit was present in these meetings in great abundance. During a Sunday morning service held in the schoolhouse, Sidney Rigdon announced that instead of the normal preaching service, the time would be occupied by the members of the Presidency and the Twelve. This proved to be a particularly moving worship experience, in which the gift of tongues was manifest "like the rushing of the mighty wind." Before the end of the service, Phelps had formulated and scribbled on the back of an envelope the words of a hymn which caught up that Pentecostal experience and forecast that which was to come.

The hymn, originally with six stanzas, was set to a stirring old English tune, "Paraclete" (which, appropriately, means "Holy Spirit" or "Comforter"), taught to the choir, and used as an anthem at the dedication service for the temple. At the end of the service, Joseph Smith spoke to the congregation and offered a prayer of dedication. His prayer ended with these words: "Help us by the power of thy Spirit, that we may mingle our voices with those bright seraphs around thy throne with acclamation of praise, singing hosanna to God and the Lamb;...and let thy Saints shout aloud for joy. Amen and Amen." The new hymn was then sung by the choir, and it is recorded that as the service concluded, President Rigdon brought brief closing remarks and offered a prayer that was "ended with loud acclamations of Hosanna! Hosanna! Hosanna to God and the Lamb, Amen, Amen, and Amen!"

W. W. Phelps is the author of three other hymns in *Hymns of the Saints*. These include "Redeemer of Israel" (*HS* 313), discussed later in this chapter; *HS* 64, "O Jesus, the Giver of All We Enjoy"; and *HS* 194, "Earth with Her Ten Thousand Flowers."

53 Hallelujah! Hallelujah!
text and tune by William Graves

During the final stages of the preparation of this manuscript, William Graves died at his home in Mississipi. He had been involved in music all his life. After graduating from Graceland College, his academic work culminated in an Ed.D. from the University of Colorado in 1963. His career as a teacher of instrumental music included eighteen years in the public schools of Missouri, Iowa, and Mississippi; seven years on the Graceland College music faculty; three years with the Tennessee State Department of Education; and seventeen years on the faculty of the Mississippi University for Women until his retirement in 1981. He was recognized as a leader in the field of music education in Mississippi.

This hymn of praise is one of a limited number to have been written entirely, both text and tune, by one person. William Graves was an individual who cultivated the skills necessary to create in both realms. His sensitivity to beauty and to the power and majesty of the Eternal Creator has resulted in this stately expression of adoration. He has left us his testimony of the creation of this hymn:

> It was a Sunday morning on the campus at Graceland College. The snow was gone, the only remaining vestige of winter was a cool breeze. Grass turning green, tree buds bursting open, an azure sky, and brilliant sunlight. The fragrance of spring filled the air. These were the sights that greeted me as I left my studio in Marietta Hall. Standing transfixed, taking in the beauty that lay before me, I felt gratitude and joy that we had been so richly blessed by our Heavenly Father. In the spirit of the moment, I sang the words that became the first verse of the hymn: "Hallelujah! Hallelujah! Sing the great Jehovah's praise; angel voices join with mortal, help the joyful anthem raise."
>
> Returning to my studio, I wrote those words and the melody that came with them. The second and third verses took a bit longer, and more time was spent on developing the harmony. This was in reality my hymn of praise.

58 Now in This Moment
text by Richard and Barbara Howard

Richard and Barbara Howard have served the RLDS Church for many years. Both retired in 1995, Barbara as a Herald House editor and Richard as World Church historian. They have been collaborating on assignments since 1952, when they worked together on a Zion's League summer production of the play "Green Pastures" in Independence, Missouri. They were married the following year. Both graduated from Graceland College and went on to graduate study. Richard received his M.A. in history from the University of California–Berkeley and began a teaching career before accepting church appointment in 1962. Barbara has done graduate studies at Saint Paul School of Theology, the University of Missouri–Kansas City, and the University of Kansas. She was a member of the committee that produced *Hymns of the Saints*.

Both of the Howards have contributed eminently to church literature through numerous books as well as articles in the *Saints Herald*. In recent years, their contribution has included the writing of hymns, some of which, like this one, have been collaborations. As is often the case, the hymn, "Now in This Moment," was written for a specific occasion and has since found its way into wider use. During the summer of 1978, a reunion for appointees and their families was held at Graceland College. One of the services was to include several testimonies and was given the theme "Our Story." The well-known Fanny Crosby hymn came to mind with its refrain, "This is my story, this is my song, praising my Savior all the day long." Crosby's verses did not seem appropriate, however, so the authors together penned the new verses, while changing the refrain to the inclusive "our." This hymn, with its lilting rhythm, has become a favorite of many and is often referred to by the memorable first line of its refrain, "This is our story." It gives a sense of perspective to the past, the present, and the future of our lives. Richard and Barbara have said of the hymn, "It is our testimony that God is creating, with us, new life in every moment of our faith journey."

69 Creation Flows Unceasingly
text by Barbara J. Higdon

Here is a hymn by a widely known educator and minister in the contemporary church. Barbara McFarlane Higdon graduated from Graceland College in 1949 and became its president thirty-five years later. In the intervening period, she obtained her Ph.D. in English and speech from the University of Missouri and served on the teaching faculties of three colleges and universities, including Graceland. She came to the Graceland presidency after ten years as dean of faculty at Park College. Since becoming president emerita of Graceland, she has continued to serve the college, the church, and the wider international community in numerous ways. Her many current activities include heading the development of the Peace Center at the Independence Temple, and serving as a board member of the SS Cyril and Methodius Foundation in Sofia, Bulgaria, the foundation that supports the Bulgarian student exchange program with Graceland. She has contributed a significant number of books and articles to the literature of the church.

Barbara was a member of the committee that produced *Hymns of the Saints*. She offers us the following insight into the thoughts expressed in her hymn, "Creation Flows Unceasingly":

Two great scriptures of the Old Testament describing creation connect for me with those mysterious passages in the Doctrine and Covenants that speak of intelligence and light, of being and becoming, of spirit and element. The image of the morning stars shouting for joy at the dawn of creation in Job is for me a "big bang" more profound than the one hypothesized by scientists today. The creation of male and female in the image of God found in Genesis proclaims a unity among humankind that rises above our struggle to identify and understand ourselves as men and women. Latter day revelation proclaims the intelligent energy of divine creation which produces the infinite variety of forms in which we humans take such immense delight. At the same time the revealed word proposes an enveloping unity of all creation—spirit as well as matter—and a mysterious purpose known only to the creator. The Doctrine and Covenants speaks of an infinite, dynamic process of creation in which everything has a part. For many years a sense of awe that goes beyond words has grown within me as I have contemplated these concepts. I believe that my being in some marvelous way is joined with all persons who have ever lived and with all the rest of creation in the ongoing creative labor of God—to bring to pass our immortality and eternal life.

The familiar tune "Duke Street" is generally attributed to John Hatton, a native of Lancashire, England. It was first printed in a collection of hymn tunes published in Scotland in 1793, and is said to be named for a street on which the author once lived.

106 How Shall We Come Before You Now
text by Geoffrey F. Spencer

Geoffrey Spencer (see *HS* 1 for biographical information) has given us a hymn that prompts us to ask ourselves why we come together in worship, and just what it is we can bring to that experience. It asks the question, "Is not whatever we have to bring, in fact, really God's in the first place?" The questions of the first three stanzas are answered by the last. The only thing we have to bring that is truly ours is our own brokenness and contrition. But that is all we need to bring; that is enough to begin the redeeming process of the renewal of our spirits.

Brother Spencer has expressed the thoughts that led to the writing of this hymn. He says,

I have long felt the value of a hymn text which would address the question of grace by frankly acknowledging the human situation, in terms of the pride and self-centeredness which prompts human beings to see themselves as the center of their universe and their gifts or achievements as grounds for self-congratulations. So the text draws attention to two basic ideas: (1) the frailty of human nature, and yet (2) the power of a broken heart and contrite spirit, which is, as it were, our gift to God, which is wholly acceptable, and the ground of the new life in the Spirit.

This hymn is sung to a tune written in 1840 by Charles Hutcheson for use in the church where he worshiped, St. George's in Glasgow, Scotland. It is named after the Scottish village, Stracathro.

110 I Lift My Soul to Thee, Lord
text by Alan D. Tyree

Alan Tyree served the RLDS Church as a full-time appointee minister for forty-two years until his retirement in 1992. Before becoming a general officer of the church he served in North America and French Polynesia. For sixteen years he was a member of the Council of Twelve Apostles, and during the last ten years before retirement he was a member of the First Presidency. For eight years, until April 1994, he chaired the Architecture and Art Committee for the Independence Temple. Brother Tyree possesses a rich background in music, including a degree from the University of Iowa, where he majored in music with minors in education and religion. He is a skilled performer on bassoon and saxophone, as well as the other woodwind instruments, and continues these musical pursuits in retirement.

Brother Tyree was a member of the committee that produced *Hymns of the Saints*. As was the case with others on the committee, he clearly saw the need for more hymns that would express certain key concepts, and frequently set his own hand to filling those needs. This hymn resulted from the felt need for additional hymns in the category of "Repentance and Forgiveness." It is an adaptation of Psalm 25, which begins, "Unto Thee, O Lord, do I lift up my soul."

The author has commented on Psalm 25:

This psalm is a confession of sin and a plea for help. It deals with the burdens of shame and guilt, and looking to God for salvation. It evidences repentance, and begs forgiveness. The hymn text has attempted to preserve these qualities in a confessional statement which is poetic and easily understood.

The tune, "Vigil," is from a Swedish folk melody.

112 Heavenly Father, We Adore Thee
text by Mark H. Forscutt

This hymn of praise has been sung by the church for many years. It is a congregational prayer for forgiveness and for the blessing of the Lord as we are drawn together in worship. The life of the author of these verses, Mark Forscutt, an important church leader during the last century, has been discussed under *HS* 2. Roy Cheville comments about this hymn:

> The prayer "Let no spirit false deceive us" was reminiscent of the years he [Forscutt] sincerely and yet mistakenly followed those who led him into spiritual distress. The phrase "few in number" recalled the time when as a young man he had gone with the small fellowship of British Saints, even at the price of ostracism. He knew this again in the [eighteen] sixties when he found his way into the Reorganization just then getting on its feet.... The hymn breathes the warm piety of the man who knew his God intimately.

The tune, "Omni Die," first appeared in Germany in 1631 as a setting for one of the many *Marienlieder* songs about the Virgin Mary, which were popular at that time. The harmonization is by the nineteenth-century English church musician William Smith Rockstro.

122 With Eyes of Faith
text by Evan A. Fry
tune by Franklyn S. Weddle

For many years, Evan Fry was the radio voice of the church. Born into the appointee family of Charles Fry (see *HS* 332), he lived in several cities of the Midwest before settling down in Independence, Missouri, in 1912. His musical training came in addition to his formal schooling, and included private piano lessons and years of singing in various choirs. He did editorial work on the 1930 *Saints' Hymnal* and began to do radio work for the church as well until the

Depression eliminated his position. Evan was able to find commercial work in radio in nearby Kansas for several years until the church was in a position to call him back to Independence. He became the director of the church's broadcasting department and later was appointed as the official radio minister.

For many years the church broadcast short devotional programs live from a radio transmitter at the Stone Church. It is said that on more than one occasion, during times of severe winter weather, Evan was the only person able to get to the studio in time for the broadcast. His unusual range of talents enabled him to single-handedly start up the equipment, play the theme music on the organ, sing the solo to his own accompaniment, and preach the morning sermon! While in the radio office, he became a close friend of the music director, Franklyn S. Weddle. The two men collaborated on a number of projects, including several hymns and hymn tunes. Each respected the outstanding gifts of the other.

"With Eyes of Faith" is a humble expression of our basic sinfulness and our need, through faith, to allow the atonement of Christ to do its work of forgiveness and perfection within us. Teamed, as it is, with Franklyn Weddle's tune, it is one of the most sincere and effective hymns of faith to come out of the Restoration movement. (See *HS* 291 for more information on Franklyn Weddle.)

Evan Fry was one of the church's most prolific writers of both hymn texts and hymn tunes. *Hymns of the Saints* includes no less than eleven hymns that have resulted from his skill and devotion.

130 How Gentle God's Commands
tune by Arthur Hicks Mills

This beloved hymn comes from an eighteenth-century English clergyman, Philip Doddridge, a friend of both Isaac

Watts and John Wesley. It is sung by other churches, but the Reorganized church sings it to a tune by one of its own, Arthur Hicks Mills. Arthur, the son of musician Henry R. Mills (see *HS* 386), was active in a variety of leadership ministries in Independence, Missouri, early in this century, including membership on the high council of the old Independence Stake. But it is for his contributions to the music of the church that he is remembered most. He played first the old reed organ and subsequently the pipe organ at the Stone Church. He taught piano at Graceland and in Independence, and was a member of the committee that compiled the *Saints Hymnal* of 1895.

While working on the earlier hymnal, *Saints' Harmony*, Mark Forscutt (see *HS* 24) often visited in the Mills home in an effort to encourage Henry to write some tunes for that collection. Young Arthur asked if he could try his hand, so Forscutt gave him five texts for which a new tune was needed. This text was one of them. Arthur Mills is also the composer of the tune "Hicks" used with *HS* 3 ("With Thankful Hearts We Meet") and *HS* 365 ("Lord God, We Meet in Jesus' Name"). Arthur's brother, Frank Mills, is the author of the fine Christmas hymn "Newborn of God" (see *HS* 247).

131 Unmoved by Fear, My Praise Is Due
text by Joseph Smith III

We are fortunate to have several hymns from the pen of the beloved prophet who led the reorganization of the church. Perhaps young Joseph's sensitivity and depth of spirit were honed during his boyhood days in Nauvoo and his struggles over the decision to follow his martyred father as leader of the church. This hymn was written during the early years of his presidency and expresses the deep faith of one who had found a personal relationship with his God and Savior. Roy Cheville has said that Joseph III "sensed the foundation of prophetic ministry was his own personal communion with his God. The wholesomeness of his faith is shown in the hymn."

This hymn can teach us something about true praise. The praise the author offers to his God is not praise prompted by fear, but rather that praise "taught" by an all-encompassing sense of love. The only fear expressed is the fear of unworthiness to walk beside his "noblest Friend." The final prayer of the hymn is an expression of faith: "On thee, my Savior, I depend."

The tune, "Park Street," was written early in the nineteenth century by Frederick Marco Antonio Venua, one of the earliest members of England's Royal Society of Musicians. It has also been sung with the hymn, "Awake, My Soul and with the Sun."

We sing three other hymns written by Joseph Smith III. One is another hymn of faith and trust, *HS* 146, "Tenderly, Tenderly, Lead Thou Me On," and the other two are benedictory hymns, *HS* 482, "Let Us Breathe One Fervent Prayer," and *HS* 490, "Lord, Let Thy Blessing Rest in Peace." Each is discussed elsewhere in this chapter. Both *HS* 146 and 482 use tunes written by Joseph's good friend Norman W. Smith, who had moved with his family to Lamoni, Iowa, to be a part of the growing church community in Decatur County (see *HS* 8).

140 Awake! Ye Saints of God, Awake!
text by Eliza R. Snow

This historic hymn grew out of the turmoil of the early days of Latter Day Saintism. Its author, Eliza Snow, was one of the outstanding women of the early Restoration. Born in Massachusetts, she moved with her family to Ohio in 1806, where she came in contact with the Restoration and was baptized in 1835. The next year the family moved to Far West,

Missouri, and then to the settlement at Adam-ondi-Ahman, from which they were subsequently driven by those who opposed the church. The family settled in Nauvoo, where Eliza returned to her earlier occupation of teaching school. She joined the exodus to Utah in 1846 and is said to have walked nearly all the way, driving her team of oxen. In 1849, she was married to Brigham Young, and her brother Lorenzo Snow succeeded Wilford Woodruff in 1898 as president of the Utah church.

The hymn's references to "Zion's bondage," "the widow's tear," "the orphan's moan," "the blood of those that slaughtered lie," and the gathering of the tempests were surely the heartbroken expressions of a people who had been driven from their settlements in Missouri and who had gone through the terrible massacre at Haun's Mill. Nevertheless, the hymn looks forward to a better day, a "glorious scene...drawing nigh" when the fierce storm will pass by. It ends with an urgent call that is as appropriate today as it was in those difficult times, the timeless call to the church to "awake to union and be one."

As noted previously with *HS* 69, the tune "Duke Street" is generally attributed to the eighteenth-century English composer, John Hatton.

142 A Mighty Fortress Is Our God
Martin Luther, revised by Alan D. Tyree

This, of course, is one of the great hymns of Christendom. Its famous tune was discussed in the preceding chapter. Its text is mentioned here because Alan Tyree (see *HS* 110) has made significant revisions in the version published in *Hymns of the Saints*. He explains the purpose of these revisions in the following narrative:

> [This hymn] is a revision of a part of the traditional English translation of Martin Luther's words. I found considerable difficulty with the

theological problems contained in the text, with obsolete imagery and archaic idioms, and rather poor English syntax, even allowing for poetic license. In stanza 1, the last five phrases read in the original:

> For still our ancient foe
> Doth seek to work us woe;
> His craft and power are great,
> And, armed with cruel hate,
> On earth is not his equal.

Note how the idea that Satan is so powerful that he is unequaled on earth contrasts with Christ's statement: "All power has been given unto me in heaven and in earth. Go ye therefore...." There are many implications of this theological error, not the least of them being motiviation by fear of Satan rather than identification with Christ. I substituted the following:

> We have no foe to fear—
> Our strength, our help is near.
> Whose power is manifest
> To lay our fears to rest.
> On earth Christ has no equal.

Alan Tyree also changed the last five phrases of stanza 2 as follows, an effort, in his own words, to "assist our appreciation of the grace of God which the opening lines of the stanza seem to suggest," and to update "archaic expression which communicates little to contemporary Christians." The original is printed below on the left, with the revision on the right.

Dost ask who that may be?	Such love does Christ reveal
Christ Jesus, it is he;	That all our wounds can heal;
Lord Sabaoth his name,	By his unbounded grace
From age to age the same,	We stand before God's face;
And he must win the battle.	Our Lord has won the battle.

In stanza 3, the last five phrases originally read as they are printed below, on the left. Brother Tyree has made an effort to improve the expression of the same ideas in his revision, printed on the right.

Let goods and kindred go,	If all we love and claim—
This mortal life also;	Our loved ones, wealth, and fame—

The body they may kill:	Were from us stripped away,
God's truth abideth still;	Our God does not betray!
His kingdom is forever.	His kingdom is forever.

146 Tenderly, Tenderly, Lead Thou Me On
text by Joseph Smith III
tune by Norman W. Smith

This is another gentle hymn of faith and trust written by the first president and prophet of the Reorganization, Joseph Smith III (see *HS* 131), when he was nearly sixty years of age. For almost thirty years he had carried the day-to-day burdens of a church working to find its own identity and establish foundations for growth. Through his leadership, a little band who remained in the Midwest after the death of his father had become a viable church organization. In this hymn we catch a glimpse of a prophet who walked closely with God, whose inner strength and humility led him to be known among the Saints as "Joseph the Beloved."

In addition to bearing the onerous cares of the church, Joseph III was no stranger to personal trials and suffering. The loss of two children was followed by the death of his first wife, Emmaline. These lines from a poem he wrote during this time reveal both the depth of his grief and the remarkable comfort he derived from his faith in God.

> Beneath the darkest cloud
>   God's hand I see...
> Through blinding tears, thy smile,
>   My God, I see.

Years later, he was to lose his eldest living son, David Carlos, and a few years later his youngest daughter, Bertha Azuba, was killed in a tragic school playground accident. In his memoirs, he recalls,

My wife was heart-broken, and I must confess to a spirit of great rebellion. Constantly recurred the question, wrung from an agonized heart: "Why, oh why?...Here I was,...away from home, at work among his people, trusting my all to [Him].... And in spite of this sincere labor and consecration on my part, He has allowed the dearest human treasure of my family to be taken from me, and in such a pitiful way."

When his grief became almost unbearable, there ensued a spiritual experience that helped to reconcile him to his loss. The prophet was not to be spared the sorrows of this life, but through the grace of a loving God he was enabled to emerge from these times of trial offering a greater and deeper ministry to his people. The authors of *Stories of Our Hymns* have expressed the belief that this hymn grew out of those life experiences. They have written:

Prepared by the varied experiences of a long life in the service of God [Joseph] wrote the hymn beginning: "Tenderly, tenderly, lead thou me on; On o'er the way where my Savior hath gone," knowing that way to be one of service and of suffering, under the sunlight of God's love. Now he could sing, "Ways have grown short that seemed once to be long."... Though at times, under great pressure of distress, his heart had grown weak, as had even the heart of "Him who had trodden the wine press alone," yet he knew the infinite tenderness of the One who would be holding his hand. With gladness he could join in the triumphant song:
"Tenderly, tenderly, leading me on."

Stories of Our Hymns tells how Joseph Smith met his friend Norman W. Smith (see *HS* 8) in front of the old Brick Church in Lamoni one Sunday morning and asked him to write music to go with these words. At first Norman questioned whether he would be equal to the task, but Joseph is said to have replied, "You write the music to suit yourself and everyone will be satisfied." With Norman's tune, this hymn first appeared in the 1903 *Zion's Praises* and has been sung by the Saints ever since.

150 Lord, in This Hour

text by Naomi Russell
tune by Dale Rider

Writing has been a part of Naomi Russell's life for as long as she can remember. She began writing poetry in response to assignments by her third-grade teacher, and by age sixteen she was writing for the church's weekly radio program. When editor Leonard Lea used one of her poems in the *Saints Herald*, it presaged a rich career of forty-three years as assistant editor at Herald House, the church's publishing company. During that time she produced hundreds of articles and books, but, she observes, "Of all these things that have gone to press, the words most frequently read are, I believe, those in *Hymns of the Saints*." She has authored or coauthored seven hymns in that collection.

Naomi has shared a deeply personal testimony of the creation of this hymn, which begins with the words, "Lord, in this hour enable us to see the breadth and depth of thine eternity." Naomi explains, "I wrote this when we knew that our daughter would soon die of cancer. She had just finished getting her master's degree and was looking forward to teaching public school music when her affliction began. Three years later she passed away, leaving her husband and two young sons."

Especially when seen in the context of their origin, the words of this hymn communicate a powerful testimony of the search for the perspective of the Eternal, where both life and death are seen as part of the natural flow of God's creation. "But life and light go on unendingly—one bright mosaic known alone to thee."

The tune, "Wiesbaden," was written by Dale Rider of Independence, Missouri. Dale is a graduate of Graceland College, where his studies included organ and composition. He is presently a staff organist at the Auditorium and Temple, and is active in the composing and publishing of music. He and his wife, Twyla, have studied modern methods of music engraving with experts in Germany, and these skills were put to use in the work of engraving the music for *Hymns of the Saints*. As a result of this excellent work, the hymnal has received recognition for the fine quality of its printed music.

151 Every Good and Perfect Gift
text by Geoffrey F. Spencer
tune by Mark H. Forscutt

This is one of two hymns in *Hymns of the Saints* that matches new words to this historic tune. The stirring tune, "Emerald," was written by Mark Forscutt (see *HS* 2), a musician and prominent church leader during the late nineteenth century, and sung with the words, "Burst, ye emerald gates, and bring to my raptured vision...." Forscutt was also the composer of the tune, "Blest Be Thou, O God of Israel" (*HS* 24), discussed earlier, and the author of two hymn texts, "Met in Thy Sacred Name, O Lord" (*HS* 2) and "Heavenly Father, We Adore Thee" (*HS* 112).

Geoffrey Spencer (see *HS* 1) has crafted a text for this tune that beautifully relates the virtues of faith, hope, and charity or love. He comments, "I have always been strongly impressed by the linking of the three 'cardinal' virtues, as in Romans 13, and felt that a text which incorporated the three in one hymn would be a helpful addition to our hymnody." He notes that, although writing rarely comes easily for him, in this instance,

> ...the ideas and language seemed to flow fairly freely, perhaps because the tune allowed for more flexibility in matching the words to the music. Although the several ideas had been in the forefront of my consciousness for some time they came together very quickly during a worship service centered in the idea of hope.

Brother Spencer believes the concept of hope deserves more of our attention as it relates not only to assurance, but ultimately to the vital concept of freedom itself. Indeed, in the words of the hymn, "Freedom soars on wings of hope."

158 There's an Old, Old Path
text by Vida E. Smith
tune by Audentia Smith Anderson

More than ninety years ago a minister in the Lamoni Congregation chose a familiar passage for his Sunday morning sermon, and in it a member of the congregation that day found an unusual measure of inspiriation. The passage was from Jeremiah 6:16: "Thus saith the Lord, Stand ye in the ways, and see, and ask for the old paths, where is the good way, and walk therein."

The sermon and the name of the minister have long been forgotten, but the words Vida Smith jotted in her church school quarterly during the service that morning in 1903 have become one of the most beloved hymns of the RLDS Church. "The Old, Old Path" is a hymn that speaks simply, but deeply and eloquently, of the treasure of close companionship with good friends and with the Master.

Vida E. Smith was born in 1865 at Nauvoo, the daughter of Alexander Hale and Elizabeth Kendall Smith. The family had moved to Harrison County, Missouri, south of Lamoni, to join the church colony as it developed in that area. In 1886 she married Heman C. Smith, apostle and church historian.

Mary Audentia Smith Anderson, daughter of Joseph III and Bertha Madison Smith, was born in 1872 at Plano, Illinois. With the church's "first family," she moved to Lamoni and lived for many years at Liberty Hall on the west outskirts of town. She was married in 1891 to Benjamin M. Anderson, superintendent of the mechanical department of Herald Publishing House at Lamoni.

Audentia studied music at Western Normal College in Shenandoah, Iowa, and at Graceland College in Lamoni. The two women were cousins, granddaughters of Joseph and Emma Smith. They were both members of the *Zion's Praises* committee, and collaborated on several hymns, including the first hymn in that hymnal, "One Day When Fell the Spirit's Whisper."

The story of the writing of "The Old, Old Path" has been told in several accounts by Vida Smith. The following excerpts are taken from *The Saints' Herald Conference Daily* and *Stories of Our Hymns:*

> It was after a tedious Sunday school session one Sabbath, a glorious summer day.... I came up from the primary rooms in the Brick Church in Lamoni and seated myself in the usual place on the north side of the church. A slight breeze moved the branches of the trees near the window; birds flitted about and called or sat on some swaying branch, singing in the Sabbath softness; the choir sang and someone prayed—all as usual. The minister read his text, that old favorite...about finding the old paths and walking therein.
>
> He soon faded from my realization as my eyes rested on the swaying branches of the trees and the soft clouds against the blue sky, and I felt the nearness of congenial friends. I felt at home in the house of God, and I felt at ease before his mercy seat. The glory of the message of the ancient prophet flooded my soul and, opening my quarterly, I wrote on the flyleaf the words of the song exactly as they appear in the hymnal.

With the encouragement of a friend, the author showed the lines to her cousin, Audentia, who employed her musical training to compose the tune to which they have always been sung.

The old Brick Church burned in 1931, and when in recent years the new church was built slightly north of the old site, the wooded spot to which the author refers in her story was cleared. A footpath had wound through that wooded area and over a small stone bridge and, while not specifically mentioned by Vida Smith, this path for many years had become associated with the hymn. Recently, members of the church in Lamoni have constructed an approximate recreation of the old path, and the surrounding area has been developed into a park that commemorates the writing of this beloved hymn.

164 God of Smallness, God of Greatness
text by Naomi Russell
tune by William Graves

This is a short little hymn set to a stately tune, thus serving as a graphic illustration of the idea it expresses. Like the hymn "The Old, Old Path," it was inspired by a sermon and written during a worship service. In this case, the sermon was by Harold Neal, former music director of the church, who was expressing the idea that the greatness of God can be found both in the unfathomable small things of creation and also in the limitless expanses of that same creation. These four lines are a stimulating summation of what was said in the sermon that day.

The hymn is sung to the tune "Hymn of Praise," which William Graves originally wrote for his hymn "Hallelujah! Hallelujah!" (see *HS* 53).

183 Lord, Lead Me by Your Spirit
text by Eric L. Selden

Eric Selden makes his home in Australia, where he is retired from a career as a well-known accountant. His years of ministry have included service as a pastor and counselor to the bishop of the church in that country. He has written poetry all his life, but began writing hymns about 1968. When then-church music director Franklyn Weddle visited Australia that year, Selden says he saw this as "an opportunity to 'bail him up' about many archaic expressions and downright bad theology in many of the hymns in *The Hymnal*." Weddle encouraged him to write the kind of hymns he felt were needed but warned him that he might have to "write about 500 before one of lasting quality came along." Selden responded by writing many hymns, theme songs, and words for special occasions over the years that followed, and two of the fruits of his gifts have been included in *Hymns of the Saints*.

The hymn, "Lord, Lead Me by Your Spirit," was written in one sitting and unaltered except for two minor corrections. While the impetus for its creation in 1975 has been long forgotten by the author, he affirms that the writing process was a "very good, albeit brief, experience, the kind we all have on rare occasions when our minds are illuminated." The tune, "Holy Wings," arranged from a Swedish folk meoldy, is also used with *HS* 1.

186 Creator of Sunrises

text by Evelyn Maples

Evelyn Maples grew up in Springfield, Missouri, where, she says, "I was encouraged by family and teachers to continue my love affair with words. The small RLDS congregation on East Dale Street loved into being the talents of the small ones, and this became increasingly important after the death of my mother when I was eight years old."

She continues, "I submitted my first poem to the *Saints Herald* about 1942; others followed, along with children's stories inspired by my three, for eleven years. By a circuitous route, I arrived in Independence from Arizona in 1953 and worked at Herald House for almost 28 years." She served as copy editor during the years when *Hymns of the Saints* was being compiled, and although she wrote four hymns for the collection herself, she modestly maintains that her greatest contribution was in refining hymn texts for other contributors. "Creator of Sunrises" was solicited by the committee in their search for more hymns depicting God as creator. The beautiful imagery used by the author has placed this hymn among the favorites of many worshipers. The closing lines provide an apt example: "Restore us to order of sunrise and trees, and love that can make the earth grander than these."

The tune used with this text is of folk origin, first published under the name "Charity" in Ingalls's *Christian Harmony* of 1805. This was a three-part setting with the melody in the middle voice. In 1801 it was set with the text of an anonymous folk hymn known as "I Love Thee." The first stanza of that hymn began, "O Jesus my Savior, to Thee I submit."

199 He Lives in Us! Immortal King!
text by Linda E. Coffman
tune by Frances Hurst Booth

Linda E. Coffman grew up in Council Bluffs, Iowa. She studied organ during her high school years and also while attending Graceland College and Iowa State University. After receiving a degree in English, she taught for several years in Iowa and Massachusetts. During the time this hymn was written, Linda was music director and organist at the Central Congregation in Council Bluffs. She and her family now attend the Northwest Congregation in Omaha, where she continues to minister through music as well as through teaching the senior high church school class. Linda has shared her testimony of the writing of this hymn:

"He Lives in Us!" was written on April 29, 1980. Its writing was a growing experience for me which I will always treasure. [As I awoke one morning, I found] the phrases "He lives in us, for us, and through us" literally pounding within me. They fit a tune which had come to me earlier for which I had no words. I arose and began to write the text, what little I had, and the tune on paper. My young boys, then three and seven, were miraculously still sleeping. At about 9:00 a.m., I knew that time was running short, and I felt strongly that the rest of the words needed to be written down, but I didn't yet know what they were. I prayed that I might be able to complete these thoughts. At 9:04, the next time I looked at the clock, there were three finished verses down in my handwriting, expressing thoughts about our oneness with God, our worth in his sight, and the tremendous joy which can be ours as we recognize and respond in obedience to his Spirit as it lives and moves within us. The writing looked as if I had spent a long time on it, with corrections in punctuation and work on rhyming in the margin.

The hymn answers, for me, the important theological question of how we can be one with God. It expresses the total joy of persons as they discover their worth, respond to his call, and acknowledge his Spirit being alive in and through them and their world.

The tune, "Hurst," was written by Frances Hurst Booth during the summer of 1954 while studying church music at the University of Colorado. It was originally set with the text, "Awake, my soul, stretch every nerve," by the eighteenth-century English clergyman Philip Doddridge, and was paired with this text in *The Hymnal* of 1956.

Frances Booth was born in Chicago, Illinois, to parents who were both converts to the RLDS Church from different denominations. She studied piano as a child, and by age eight was playing for Sunday school worship. She served for many years as pianist and organist for the Washington, D. C., congregation, and is continuing this area of ministry during her retirement years in Arizona.

205 My Children, "Hear Ye Him," My Word
text by Alan D. Tyree

Alan Tyree (see *HS* 110) bears a very personal testimony concerning this hymn. Here is what he has written about the experience of its creation:

"My Children, 'Hear Ye Him,' My Word" was my first hymn. It came as a result of a challenge. Frequently I had complained to the hymnal committee about the lack of hymns proclaiming the concept that the gospel is life lived, and not some statement of words about that life. Usually, when you hear the word, "gospel," the images that come to mind are the Four Gospels, or a statement of doctrines, teachings, and beliefs that can be published, spoken, preached, and recorded—all verbal expressions. For some time, I had been asking the committee to try to find a hymn or hymns which would treat the concept of "gospel" more adequately. Finally some of the members started telling me that I would have to write it myself because they couldn't find it anywhere.

I felt considerable inspiration in writing this text, and have usually been unable to sing it or recite it aloud because of deep emotional involvement. It is based on Scripture, the opening verses of John's Gospel. It should be noted that it is one of a very few hymns that are God's words to us, rather than our speaking to God or to ourselves.

The tune, "Rockingham," was first published in 1790. Its composer, Edward Miller, was organist at Doncaster Parish Church in England, and named the tune after his patron and friend, the Marquis of Rockingham, who served twice as prime minister of Britain. The tune has been associated with Isaac Watts's hymn "When I Survey the Wondrous Cross."

206 Come, Thou, O King of Kings
text by Parley P. Pratt, revised by Alan D. Tyree

This hymn originated from the pen of one of the great missionaries of the Latter Day Saint movement. Parley Parker Pratt was born in Burlington, New York, in 1807 and left home at the age of nineteen. During the winter of 1826–27 he cleared some land in a forested area west of Cleveland and built himself a log cabin. It was during this time that he came in contact with Sidney Rigdon, at that time a free-lance preacher. Pratt became so enthusiastic about Rigdon's group that he sold everything and went to New York to preach. While in New York, he saw a copy of the Book of Mormon and began to read it. He was so moved by its message that he traveled to Palmyra to talk with Hyrum Smith. In a matter of a few days, on September 1, 1830, Pratt was baptized by Oliver Cowdery and ordained an elder immediately.

Parley Pratt was a true pioneer of the Restoration. He was a part of many of the first missionary efforts of the young movement. The work in the Kirtland area was begun as a result of Pratt's conversion of his friend, Sidney Rigdon, who would later serve in the First Presidency with Joseph Smith. Pratt and his wife moved to Missouri as a part of the first gathering movement, and he was called into the first Council of Twelve in February 1835. After the death of Joseph and Hyrum Smith, Pratt joined the exodus westward to the Salt Lake Valley. Parley P. Pratt is also the author of the baptism tune, "O God in Heaven, We Believe" (*HS* 356), and the confirmation hymn, "Behold Thy Sons and Daughters, Lord" (*HS* 361).

After so many years, it is to be expected that some of the expressions contained in the church's early hymnody would need to be revised in light of contemporary language and understandings. Alan Tyree (see *HS* 110) has made this revision of Parley P. Pratt's hymn with a view to updating some of its theological concepts. In the last stanza, the phrase, "While all the *chosen race*" becomes the less exclusive "While saints of every race." In the same stanza, "The *heathen* nations bow the knee" becomes "The *thankful* nations bow the knee."

The tune, "Lenox," was written by the American composer Lewis Edson, who was a blacksmith in Massachusetts in the late eighteenth century before turning to music teaching and composing.

230 Look at This Man, Born of God
translated by Hiroshi Yamada

Hiroshi Yamada was born in Sasebo, Nagasaki, Japan, and baptized in 1959 by Kisuke Sekine, after Sekine returned to Japan from attending Graceland College. Brother Yamada became one of the early members of the church in that country and helped in the formal establishment of the work there in 1961. In that same year, he came to America to attend Graceland College himself. In 1963 he accepted church appointment and became the national minister for Japan in 1966.

In the process of compiling *Hymns of the Saints*, Geoffrey Spencer asked Hiroshi to make a translation of one of the favorite hymns used by the church in Japan and submit it to the committee. He responded by choosing this hymn from the hymnal of the United Church of Christ in Japan, which is the collection used by members of the RLDS Church in that country. As a result of Hiroshi's beautiful translation of some of the poetic expressions of his distinctive culture, this hymn presents the worshiper with fresh, sincere new language describing the profound significance of the life and sacrifice of Jesus Christ.

"Mabune," which means "manger," is the tune used with the original hymn in Japan. It was written in 1930 by Seigi Abe who, like Hiroshi Yamada, was born in Japan but spent several years in the United States. Abe studied music at the New England Conservatory of Music in Boston. Upon returning to Japan, he became a noted church musician and composed numerous hymns and other sacred music.

234 Joseph, Kind Joseph
text by Naomi Russell

Naomi Russell (see *HS* 150) has written a charming new Christmas hymn in "Joseph, Kind Joseph." The three stanzas offer us, in turn, a glimpse of what might have been the personal feelings of each of the three members of the Holy Family on the night of Jesus' birth. The momentous implications of that event are imaginatively caught up in these three personal reflections, and this wider perspective is further enlarged in the lines of the refrain.

The author wrote this hymn as a Christmas greeting to share with friends in the holiday tradition, but hoped that it would someday see wider circulation in a new hymnal. She originally set the words to a tune she herself wrote, but in *Hymns of the Saints* it has been matched with a traditional Appalachian yuletide folk hymn, "Star in the East." For this hymnal, the tune has received a new harmonization by John Obetz, organist at the Auditorium and Temple.

239 Silvery Star, Precious Star
text by Elbert A. Smith
tune by Audentia Smith Anderson

Elbert Aoriul Smith, son of David Hyrum and Clara Hartshorn Smith, possessed some of the artistic temperament of his father (see *HS* 8). He appreciated beauty in its many manifestations, and he was endowed with a warm sense of humor. He contributed mightily to the publications of the church through books, articles, and poetry. He worked for many years with Herald Publishing House and served as assistant editor of the *Saints' Herald* and editor of the young people's magazine, *Autumn Leaves*. "Brother Elbert," as he was affectionately known, served as counselor in the presidencies of both Joseph III and Frederick M. Smith. In 1938, he was ordained as the presiding patriarch of the church.

The tune, "Starlight and Song," was written specifically for this poem by Elbert A. Smith's cousin, Audentia Anderson, who composed music for a number of the historic hymns of the church, including "The Old, Old Path" (see *HS* 158). The authors of *Stories of Our Hymns* have summarized the message of this venerable Christmas hymn:

This hymn, "Starlight and Song," brings before us the age-old picture that is ever new. We weep with the kneeling shepherds and rejoice with the angels "singing peace and joy and cheer." In the stillness of that night, under beaming star and chanted song we look from the baby Savior to the Savior King enthroned, feeling deep desire that by his messengers of love he will lead us to himself.

241 Sing Songs of Joy
text and tune by Pamela Robison

Pamela Lents Robison grew up with music and with the RLDS Church. As a member of a church appointee family she has lived in a variety of places. She remembers being involved in music since the age of seven years, starting with service playing on an old pump organ at the church in Nuneaton, England, when her father and mother, Don and Helen Lents, were assigned to the British Isles. She has not stopped playing since, and became a member of the Auditorium organ staff in 1969. Now living with her husband and family in Sedalia, Missouri, she plays periodically on both the Auditorium and Temple organs. She graduated from Graceland College and has further degrees in English and music composition from Central Missouri State University.

When the hymnal committee called for new hymns to be submitted for *Hymns of the Saints*, Pamela decided to write a new hymn for the Christmas season. She remembers,

> The theme that kept going through my mind was that Christmas is a time of joy, and the first phrase—"Sing songs of joy"—just crystallized. I then thought what we were singing joy about. Obviously, the first reason for Christmas joy was the birth of Jesus. Then I thought about the angels who announced the birth, the shepherds who brought their gifts, and then why we should be singing that joy today. I wanted the words to be simple and easily learned—words that even children could learn quickly.
>
> After I had the poem written, I realized that there probably was no hymn tune that would meet the necessary meter requirements of 4.5.4.4.5.—so I decided I would need to include a tune as well. Again, I wanted it to be joyful—to match the mood of the words. The tune just seemed to flow easily as I worked on it. I really did not need to go back to do much reworking of it or the harmony; in fact, the most difficult task was determining the meter at the beginning of the second system of the hymn, and how long I wanted the last note to be held.

The skills this author and musician has developed have brought ministry to many people in a variety of ways. She has made a contribution to the musical treasures of Christmas with this fresh little gem of praise, which has quickly become one of the church's most popular new hymns.

247 Newborn of God

text by Frank W. Mills

The Mills family has made a strong contribution to the heritage of Latter Day Saint hymnody. Frank Mills's father, Henry Mills (see *HS* 386), and his brother, Arthur Mills (see *HS* 130), have written hymn tunes that are discussed elsewhere in this volume. This text, which Frank Mills has written, is full of meaning and application to the needs of our present day. It presents a concept of Christmas not only wholesome but profound. It is an expression of our need for the everliving Christ, the contemporary revelation of God to humankind. Through this revelation, we can know the deepest meaning of "Immanuel"—what we can be with "God with us." With its beautiful language and imagery, Brother Mills's text is one of the most eloquent expressions we have on this theme. As Roy Cheville has observed, it is a hymn of Christmas eternal.

The composer of the tune, "Toulon," was Louis Bourgeois, a French composer and follower of John Calvin, with whom he lived in Geneva for several years. He was responsible for either composing or adapting most of the melodies to which the Calvinists sang the psalms. The Calvinists believed that "only God's word is worthy to be sung in His praise," and thus limited their singing to metrical versions of the scriptures, primarily the psalms. The best-known example of this practice is the tune "Old Hundredth," which is also attributed to Louis Bourgeois. This is the tune to which we traditionally sing "Praise God, from Whom All Blessings Flow," although, as its name implies, it was originally used to sing a metrical adaptation of Psalm 100. (See the discussion of *HS* 43 in Part II, page 39).

291 Church of Christ, in Latter Days
text and tune by Franklyn S. Weddle

It would be difficult to find a person who has had more influence on the worship of the church and on its music than Franklyn S. Weddle. He was the director of the church's first department of music, established in 1948, and served in that capacity until his retirement in 1969. He also served as director of the radio and audiovisual departments during much of that time. He was a talented musician and an effective minister and leader for the church for many years.

A native of North Dakota, Franklyn Weddle studied music at Graceland College as well as at universities in Iowa, Illinois, and Michigan. He taught music in Michigan for several years before accepting church appointment in the Kansas City area. It was not long before the task of building up the musical life of the church and the Center Place became his full-time assignment. Among other contributions, he organized the Independence Symphony Orchestra, the Community Music Association, and brought the annual *Messiah* performances to such a high level of quality that they were broadcast live on the CBS radio network for many years.

In addition to leading the compilation process for a children's hymnal and a youth hymnal, Franklyn Weddle chaired the committee that produced *The Hymnal* of 1956, the predecessor to the current hymnal of the church. For the 1956 collection, he authored and coauthored several tunes, most of which continue to be used today. This hymn, however, is the only one for which he wrote both the text and the tune.

As he worked with the committee on the 1956 hymnal, one of Franklyn's concerns was the need for more hymns on the subject of the church. His son, Claire, remembers one night when, with this concern on his heart, Franklyn awoke with words and music going through his mind. He arose and wrote out this hymn essentially as it appears today, making only one minor change the following morning. The hymn was quickly accepted by the committee and has been well used and loved by the church ever since.

Franklyn Weddle's hymn is a treasured part of his legacy. It expresses the challenge that comes to those who would be members of the body of Christ and offers a prayer that divine grace will sustain the church as it seeks to fulfill its destiny.

Hymn tunes by Franklyn Weddle in *Hymns of the Saints* include those for *HS* 30 ("Let All the World in Every Corner Sing"), *HS* 122 ("With Eyes of Faith"), and a tune for Frederick M. Smith's "Onward to Zion" (*HS* 316), replacing Stephen Foster's "Beautiful Dreamer," for which the prophet originally wrote his now-familiar text.

292 By Thy Redeeming Cross, O Lord
text by Arthur A. Oakman

This is the only hymn we have from the pen of a prominent and beloved minister of the church of the recent past. Arthur Alma Oakman was born in 1905 at Ponder's End in Enfield, England, the north London location of the church's only congregation in that great city. He was active in the church, and in 1928 visiting church leaders from headquarters were so impressed with the potential of this young man that they persuaded him to come to the United States and attend Graceland College. Arthur related how, as the ship sailed away from the port, his heart sank and he wondered what he had done in cutting himself off from family, friends, and homeland. He said that he wanted to jump off the ship and swim ashore, but the words of a hymn came forcibly to his mind: "He is calling now to battle both the aged and the youth." Thus encouraged, he went on to Graceland, where his vision of the work unto which he was called was both broadened and deepened.

Arthur was a natural musician and possessed a fine baritone voice. He was often heard in solo work and won voice competitions in both England and the United States. Arthur might have had a career in music, but he chose the ministry of the church instead. He accepted church appointment after his graduation from Graceland and in 1938, after several years of missionary and pastoral experience, was called to the Council of Twelve Apostles. He and his family were assigned without delay to the European field at a time that was to become one of the most difficult and dreadful periods in its history. They arrived in England in the summer of 1938, and Arthur visited the congregations of the church on the European continent even as the threat of war was building. In his book, *He Who Is*, he gives a graphic account of being apprehended and questioned by the Gestapo.

As World War II broke out, the Oakman family was urged by church leaders to return to the States for safety, but despite the personal dangers, they chose to stay with the people who now needed their ministry more than ever. Arthur returned to America in 1944 and continued his work in the Quorum of Twelve until 1964, when he was called to the office of patriarch evangelist. His ministry of spiritual depth and prophetic insight, his contribution to the church through numerous books and articles, and his great love of music will be remembered by all who knew him.

The hymn "By Thy Redeeming Cross" is the expression of a devoted servant of his love for Jesus Christ and his church. It speaks of the divine origins of the church and the empowering ministry it is called to give. It affirms the promise of the future as we rededicate ourselves to the cause of the kingdom.

The tune, "Belmont," is an adaptation of a melody found in W. Gardiner's *Sacred Melodies*, published in 1812.

296 Afar in Old Judea
text by Roy A. Cheville

There are many legendary individuals in the relatively brief history of the Restoration, but perhaps none who have been more influential or revered than Roy A. Cheville. He taught and inspired thousands of future leaders of the church in his role of professor of religion and campus pastor at Graceland College. Despite these onerous duties, he found time to write numerous articles, books, and hymns. Many of his hymns were written because he could not find anything that was "just right" for the carefully planned worship services of the campus congregation. In 1958 he was called to church appointment to succeed Elbert A. Smith as presiding patriarch, where his singular ministry was to be shared more directly with the church at large.

Those who were privileged to sit under Roy Cheville's preaching ministry knew it to be a strong, enthusiastic ministry that emphasized "doing." In both his speaking and his writing, he preferred words with the more active "ing" endings. His song leading was renowned for its dynamic enthusiasm, almost in the style of an evangelistic cheerleader. People naturally sang better with Roy urging them on—they had no other choice!

This hymn was written for a "Quest for Christ" series of meetings held at the Stone Church in 1953. Brother Cheville was to lead the singing, and he wanted a hymn that caught up the theme of the series—that the everliving Christ is available to all. Being unable to find a hymn that exactly caught up the theme as he understood it, he penned this text himself. The first stanza speaks of the baptism of Christ in the Jordan River and the subsequent confirmation of the Holy Spirit.

The second stanza tells of the visit of Christ to ancient America as told in the Book of Mormon. The third stanza refers to the vision of Joseph Smith in the grove, and the last stanza affirms that the Christ of the ages still lives and is available to us today.

Alexander Ewing's tune to which this hymn is sung was originally written in triple meter and first published in 1853. It appeared in the Anglican *Hymns Ancient and Modern* in 1861 as a tune for "Jerusalem the Golden."

297 The Church's Life
text by Geoffrey F. Spencer and Alan D. Tyree

This new hymn brings to the church fresh insights on what it means to be a prophetic people. "The church's life is built upon the rock of revelation" is the only hymn text selected by the hymnal committee whose authors were known at the time of its consideration. Coauthor Alan Tyree (see *HS* 110) remembers how this hymn came into being:

> We were meeting in our final committee session. The possibility of new hymns being added had come to an end. We still had need for other good hymns in certain categories, but time had run out on us. During the meeting, Geoffrey Spencer began writing something while the committee work continued. We hardly noticed what he was doing until time for a break arrived. When I saw that he was writing a hymn in a category which I also felt deeply about, I joined him in working out some of the wordings.
>
> It was our hope, I think, that this hymn might serve the church better at the time of Conference acceptance of a revelatory document than the traditional "We thank thee, O God, for a prophet."

The hymn is set to a stirring tune by A. Royce Eckhardt.

298 Fountain of All Revelation
text by Deam Ferris

This hymn is a testimony of the ultimate compatibility of science and religion, born out of the convictions of a man whose life was devoted to both. Deam Ferris was a professor of biology at Graceland College for many years. He had had teaching experience at other institutions, but was challenged by the opportunity Graceland presented to integrate his scientific background and his religious beliefs. He has said,

> On coming to Graceland, these questions came to the front...I had to think through and pray through my scientific research and my religious faith. Gradually light dawned and things began to piece together. It was out of these searchings that the hymn took shape.
>
> One Wednesday evening after a very good fellowship meeting at the college, I went home disturbed. I had hesitated to speak when so many students were wanting to participate. I felt I had a testimony that needed to be expressed. That night I tried to define more clearly what it was. Ideas kept coming back to me over and over again as I tried to sleep. The following night I had the same experience. Eventually I arose and started writing. The outstanding lines came rapidly. Tying them together took more time. In fear and trembling I took my work to Roy Cheville. It was my testimony.

The thoughts of this hymn are as timely today as they were when they were written. The tune to which they have always been sung was written by Franklyn S. Weddle, then music director for the church.

299 The Living Word of Scripture
text by Geoffrey F. Spencer

Geoffrey Spencer (see *HS* 1) has written an enlightening and expansive hymn offering a broad historical perspective of the concept of revelation. He comments,

> I believe that during my lifetime in the church I have seen a significant trend in the way we approach scripture, moving away from the emphasis upon proof-texting and more towards the recognition that the scripture becomes a medium of revelation when it enables us to experience a kinship with others who have taken the same journey on which we find ourselves. I have been impressed by the way in which the scriptures arise from the everyday experience of the faithful, and were probably not intended to become "scripture" at all. Indeed I have wondered what might

have eventuated if the writers had self-consciously set out to write "scripture." We might well have had something notably more formal, theoretical, and lacking the dynamic appeal of people who were sharing their experience and testimony.

This is why I tried to communicate the idea of living scripture by lifting up the various experience of its writers. I was wanting to communicate the understanding that it is more than information which is provided by scripture—the essential spark is its power to draw us into the sense of kinship with those who have preceded us, and whose story is continuous with ours.

The tune is the Swedish folk melody "Vigil."

301, 302 O God, Our Source of Truth
text by Alan D. Tyree

Here is a case where the hymnal committee wanted to include a specific tune in *Hymns of the Saints*, but needed an appropriate text to go with it. The tune used in 301 is "Vineyard Haven." It is a fresh and interesting contemporary tune (discussed in Part II, see page 51), although it may prove a challenging one for most congregations. Alan Tyree comments on how this text came into being: "Our chair, Harold Neal, asked us to look for texts [to set with this tune] or to consider writing a text for it. So, I literally had this tune in mind when I wrote the words." After the committee had accepted Brother Tyree's text for the tune "Vineyard Haven," he asked that it also be included with another, more familiar tune. Thus, as *HS* 302, the text is set to the music of the American composer William Henry Walter. This tune, "Festal Song," is also associated with the hymn, "Rise Up, O Saints of God."

Like *HS* 110, another hymn by the same author, this hymn is based on a scriptural text. Brother Tyree goes on to explain:

The text is based on I Corinthians 13:8–12, "...whether there be knowledge, it shall vanish away. For we know in part, and we prophesy in part.

When I was a child, I spake as a child, I understood as a child, I thought as a child; but when I became a man, I put away childish things. For now we see through a glass darkly; but then face to face; now I know in part; but then shall I know even as also I am known."

The hymn is a plea to God for divine direction, and a confession that whatever truth we now hold is fragile, limited, and useful, but in time will be superseded by more complete understanding and knowledge.

306 God Has Spoken Through the Ages
text by Evan A. Fry
tune by Charles F. Church Jr.

One of the central tenets of the RLDS Church is the belief in continuing revelation. In one of the many hymns that are an important part of his legacy to the church, Evan Fry (see *HS* 122 for more information) illuminates the concept of the contemporary revelation of Divinity throughout the ages. The scriptures in this context are understood to serve not as an end, but a beginning point in discovering the mind of God. We are each called in our own day to search for still greater truth by uniting our own intellect with the inspiration of the Holy Spirit. Stanzas two and three give particularly insightful expression to the relation between revelation, scripture, and intellect:

Through the pages of the Scriptures, God's eternal truths are shown,
But in finite words and phrases God himself cannot be known...
While we thank thee for thy Scriptures, For thy word revealed of old,
Lead us, Lord, to new revealment; Still to us new truths unfold...

Evan Fry wrote these words while he was serving on the committee for *The Hymnal* of 1956. After considerable difficulty in finding an appropriate tune for his text, he turned to his colleague in the radio department, Charles F. Church Jr., and asked if he would be willing to try his hand at writing a tune. Brother Church, a native of Lamoni, Iowa, and a grandson of Norman W. Smith (see *HS* 8), had come to the church radio department from his position as educational director for radio station KMBC in Kansas City. Before that he had had a career in music, teaching instrumental music at Bowling Green College in Ohio for many years. A woodwind specialist, he had directed bands and orchestras, as well as church choirs, and was an accomplished clarinetist. Because the hymnal committee was meeting the next day, Charles worked late into the night and was successful in obtaining the group's acceptance for his tune, which he named "Van Fleet," the maiden name of his wife. As far as is known, it was the only hymn tune he ever wrote.

307 We Thank Thee, O God, for a Prophet
text by William Fowler

William Fowler was born in Australia in 1830, the son of a British soldier and his wife, who was of Irish descent. Within a few years of the family's return to England, both of his parents died, leaving William an orphan at the age of fourteen. In the winter of 1848, he became dissatisfied with his parents' Methodist religion and accepted the invitation of a friend to attend the Latter Day Saint church in Sheffield, England. The next summer he was baptized and was ordained a priest the following year. He accepted an assignment to do missionary work and was ordained an elder in 1851.

Fowler's talents included music, literature, and handicraft. He played both the violin and the piccolo, and was a cutler by trade. He was a frequent contributer to the *Millennial Star*, the Latter Day Saint publication in England. We do not know the exact circumstances of the writing of this hymn, but it was probably written before 1863, when Fowler, his wife, and three children sailed for America. The family arrived in New York on July 25, 1863, and went on to Utah, settling in Manti, where William taught school. He died only two years later. He left to the Latter Day Saint movement this grand old hymn, which has been adopted enthusiastically by the Reorganized church and traditionally sung following the presentation of inspired counsel at World Conferences of the church.

The tune, which we know as "Prophet," was written by Caroline E. S. Norton during the Crimean War of 1854–56 in memory of an English officer who was killed in action. Sung at his funeral service, "The Officer's Funeral March," as the song was called, began with the lines, "Hark to the shrill trumpet calling, it pierces the soft summer air." The music became well-enough known in England that Fowler's poem was, and is still, sung to this tune.

309 We Limit Not the Truth of God
tune by Louise Hills Lewis

It has been said that, although this hymn text was not written by a Latter Day Saint, it should have been. In these verses, the Englishman George Rawson has caught up something of the essence of the Restoration movement's emphasis on contemporary revelation. It is a message that is ever new and ever needed. We must not bind by our limited understanding the infinite truths that wait to be revealed.

Because of the importance of the words of this hymn, it is fitting that we should sing them to a tune written by a member of the Reorganization. The name of the tune, "Hills," was the maiden name of its composer, Louise Hills Lewis. She was born in 1887 at Cedar Rapids, Iowa, and studied music as a child, including piano, organ, voice, harmony, and conducting. In later years she was to put her musical training to active use in the service of the church. In addition to this music, she wrote a number of other hymn tunes, including the tune "Confirmation," used for *HS* 354 ("Here at the Water's Brink We Stand"), and *HS* 361 ("Behold Thy Sons and Daughters, Lord").

312 Let Us Pray for One Another
text by Maurice L. Draper, based on David H. Smith

Maurice Draper's ministry through the years has combined an active, keen intellect with the ability to clearly articulate his thoughts. These gifts have been invaluable in his years of leadership to the church as a general officer, most recently as a longtime member of the First Presidency. His love of music is also evident to anyone who has heard him make references to this art in his sermons, or has seen him playing his violin in amateur orchestras. He says of this love:

> I have always been deeply stirred by music. My mother played the piano and my father (an Irish tenor) occasionally sang at public programs.... [I also remember] my own singing at the top of my voice as a child, especially such hymns as "Precious Name," which I learned before I could read. The joy of singing with congregations, choirs, and quartets has continued throughout my life to the present day.

In *HS* 312, Brother Draper has written an essentially new hymn based on an idea and several key lines of text from a historical hymn by David H. Smith, son of Joseph Smith Jr. Draper comments on how this composition came about:

> During the 1970's, those responsible for planning the Sunday morning worship services at the Walnut Gardens congregation in Blue Valley Stake invited me to plan a service in which the theme involved mutual concern by members of the church community. One of the hymns that occurred to me in relation to this theme was this hymn, number 98 in *The Hymnal* of 1956.
>
> Upon reviewing the text of the hymn, I was immediately adversely impressed by the negative tone of the first stanza:
>
>> Let us pray for one another, for the day is fading fast,
>> And the night is growing darker, while the scourge goes flaming past.
>> We can see it in the darkness, closing round our narrow way,
>> And the snares are growing thicker. For each other let us pray.
>
> [I felt that] the spirit of promise in stanzas 3 and 4 is not expressed strongly enough to overcome or even balance the dominant mood of anxiety and despair in stanzas 1 and 2. I wanted to focus attention on the

mutual concern expressed in the theme, "for each other let us pray," which closes each stanza. My respect for the faith demonstrated in the artistry of David H. Smith made me reluctant to edit his poetry, but it occurred to me that it might be appropriate to produce a revised version for a single worship service.

Having so decided, I was surprised when the phrasing produced by my editorial effort seemed to flow so smoothly. I wanted to retain the mood of prayerful concern in the original text and to add emphasis on the ideas expressed in the phrasing:

"minds and hearts may blend...others need us...in love we'll share...live for others...day is dawning."

After the hymn was successfully used at the worship service for which it was intended, several people expressed their appreciation for the spirit of the new text, and it eventually came to the attention of the hymnal committee, which has included it in place of David H. Smith's original hymn.

313 Redeemer of Israel

text by W. W. Phelps

W. W. Phelps and Parley P. Pratt are the two pioneers of the Restoration movement whose legacy includes the gift of hymns that are still sung today. When the Latter Day Saint movement was little more than a year old, William Wines Phelps read the Book of Mormon and moved his family to Kirtland, Ohio, to learn more about this new church. In Section 55 of the Doctrine and Covenants, dated June 1831, he was told that he should be baptized and ordained an elder.

Phelps had been active in political affairs; he had at one time been a candidate for lieutenant governor of New York, and he was the editor of a partisan newspaper. His background in journalism would be put to good use assisting Oliver Cowdery in the printing operation of the new movement, and he was to leave at once with Joseph Smith and Sidney Rigdon for Missouri. He constructed a building in Independence and established a printing operation there. He began publishing the *Evening and the Morning Star,* which became a lifeline for the church in communicating with many scattered members. Later, while he was engaged in the task of preparing the Book of Commandments for publication, an angry mob destroyed his home and took possession of the printing office. Phelps and others offered themselves to the mob as a ransom for the rest of the Saints, but their courageous offer was not accepted. In vain he petitioned state officials and even the president of the United States to provide protection for the group.

When the first edition of the *Evening and the Morning Star* was published in June 1832, it included a hymn that caught up both the excitement and the struggles of the movement. W. W. Phelps experienced firsthand the persecution of the early Saints and likened it, in these verses, to the tribulation of the children of Israel. In writing this hymn, he was no doubt inspired by the words of an existing hymn by Joseph Swain, which was itself inspired by the Twenty-third Psalm. The first line of that hymn was, "O Thou, in whose presence my soul takes delight." The same tune, known variously as "Beloved," "Meditation," or "Davis," was used for both hymns. Several variations of this tune exist today (see page 122). There were no less than ten stanzas in Swain's hymn, and the first three of them are clearly echoed in the lines of W. W. Phelps.

O Thou in whose presence my soul takes delight,
    On whom in affliction I call;
My comfort by day and my song in the night,
    My hope, my salvation, my all.

Where dost thou at noontide resort with thy sheep,
    To feed on the pasture of love?
For why in the valley of death should I weep,
    Alone in the wilderness rove?

O why should I wander an alien from thee,
   Or cry in the desert for bread?
My foes would rejoice when my sorrows they see,
   And smile at the tears I have shed.

W. W. Phelps's hymn is one of the important musical expressions of the young Restoration movement, and it came to find resonance in the Reorganization as well. It has become a cherished and thrilling tradition to open each World Conference with the wholehearted singing of this special hymn. Roy Cheville has called it "the song of the Saints."

314 The Cause of Zion Summons Us
text by Geoffrey F. Spencer

The hymnals of the church through the years have served to both reflect and foster the changing beliefs and theologies of the movement. (As an example, we have moved away from the concepts that led Saints for many years to preach in song to all who were not members, "We come with joy the truth to teach you...that from all error you may part.") The fact of continued theological development in the church is nowhere made more apparent than through an overview of hymns about the concept of Zion, as contained in successive hymnals of the church. In hymnals from the very early years of the church, several different images of Zion can be found, including: (1) the city of God, either in heaven or descending from heaven; (2) Enoch's perfect community; (3) a place of refuge; and (4) Independence, Missouri. Of the ninety hymns selected by Emma Smith for the first hymnal in 1835, more than one-third mention Zion or the New Jerusalem.

Newer images of Zion were to emerge during the following years, often as a response to prophetic counsel to the church. These include the concept of a city built by the Saints as a light to the world. Subsequent new hymns began to reflect the idea that Zion cannot be limited to a single geographical location and that members are to maintain interdependence with the rest of the world. This concept is still changing and developing in the church.

"The Cause of Zion Summons Us," by Geoffrey Spencer (see *HS* 1 for biographical information on the author), speaks of Zion as a vision that calls for outreach and witnesses of a future of righteousness and peace for all. It affirms that Zion is a dream to be claimed today for the sake of humankind. Embracing this concept of Zion as an active, present-day endeavor, we can sing, "The Kingdom has already come; The victory is won."

The tune, "St. Matthew," was written by William Croft, who served as organist at Westminster Abbey in the eighteenth century.

316 Onward to Zion

> text by Frederick M. Smith
> tune by Franklyn S. Weddle

This familiar hymn was written in October 1922 by the prophet-president of the church at that time. Frederick Madison Smith had been born at Plano, Illinois, in 1874. He subsequently moved with his family to Lamoni to join the new church community being established there. They lived in the large house west of town known today as "Liberty Hall." F. M. Smith entered Graceland College, enrolling in 1895 as a sophomore in its first class, and graduating as the sole member of the class of 1898. He went on to receive his Ph.D. degree in 1915 from Clark University in Massachusetts, writing his dissertation on "The Higher Powers of Man."

Under the leadership of F. M. Smith the church grew in numbers and in maturity of both doctrine and organization. He recognized the importance of music to the church and encouraged its development. These times of growth were also times of growing pains. This hymn was born out of the tensions that surfaced at some of the General Conferences during the early years of his presidency. It was a call to remember what was ultimately important and to move out toward a common goal.

When he penned these words, the prophet had been listening to the music of Stephen Foster and had set his verses to the melody of "Beautiful Dreamer." The words were sung to this music for some time, but it eventually became clear that Foster's lullaby was not appropriate to the message of challenge found in this text. Since 1950 we have used the tune written by Franklyn S. Weddle (see *HS* 291) for these verses.

332 O Lord, How Can It Be
text and tune by Charles Fry

A number of thoughts and feelings flood our minds whenever we come to the table of the Lord to partake of the sacrament of the Lord's Supper. These will necessarily include deep feelings of unworthiness and our need for repentance. As a result of that repentance, however, and through wholehearted participation in that worship experience, we receive the assurance that, through Christ, we are forgiven, cleansed, and made one with God.

These are the profound thoughts so eloquently expressed in the beautiful Communion hymn written by Charles Fry. Fry was born in the peaceful atmosphere of rural Wiltshire, England, in 1872. The rich, vibrant tradition of hymn singing in the Church of England was to nurture him in his youth. When he was thirteen, he was invited to go to America and live with an aunt and uncle in Tabor, Iowa. This was a family who were members of the Reorganization and, in less than a year, Charles had joined as well. As he grew into adulthood, he was called to priesthood responsibility, and in 1900 he accepted church appointment.

The period between 1924 and 1930 found Charles Fry and his family in Kirtland, Ohio, living in the Sidney Rigdon home across the street from the Temple. It was in this historic setting that the words of this hymn were written on December 28, 1928. Two days later, Fry called on his skill as a self-taught musician to write the music for the hymn as well. Fittingly, he named the tune, "Kirtland." Charles Fry is also the composer of the tune "Communion," written for the words of the eighteenth-century clergyman Samuel Stennett, "Here at Thy Table, Lord, We Meet" (*HS* 338).

334 We Come, Aware of Sin
                              text by Naomi Russell

341 Remembering Thy Son, O God
                              text by Naomi Russell
                              tune by Harold Neal

    This pair of hymns was written by Naomi Russell (see *HS* 150) in response to a request by the committee for the submission of new texts for use with the sacrament of the Lord's Supper. The second hymn was written by the author in an attempt to make a requested revision of the first, but ultimately the committee accepted both of them. Together they add to the variety of sincere new expressions about the significance of this sacrament and our rightful response to it.

    The tune used with *HS* 334 has been ascribed to the seventeenth-century composer, Johann Cruger. It is commonly associated with the hymn "Now Thank We All Our God." The tune, "Marnie," to which *HS* 341 is set, was written by Harold Neal, church music director and chairman of the hymnal committee during the period when *Hymns of the Saints* was compiled. It is named for the composer's wife.

    Harold Neal, a native of London, Ontario, Canada, joined the music faculty of Graceland College in 1953. He had had a musical career as a violinist and conductor in Canada, and his assignment at Graceland included work with both instruments and voices. He was chairman of the fine arts department when he was invited, in 1967, to come to Independence in anticipation of the retirement of Franklyn Weddle as director of music for the church. In 1969, Harold Neal took over the responsibility of this office, which included leadership in music and worship, and conducting the annual broadcast performance of Handel's *Messiah*. Since his retirement in 1981, he has remained active in a variety of musical endeavors and performances. In looking back on his years of service to the church, he says that giving leadership to the process of producing *Hymns of the Saints* was among the richest of all his experiences.

342 Let Us Break Bread Together
tune harmonized by Rosalee Smith Elser

No commentary on RLDS contributions to *Hymns of the Saints* can be complete without making reference to the work of Rosalee Elser. As that hymnal's Index of Composers, Arrangers, and Sources will show, no less than thirty-seven hymn tunes (and two texts) in that collection bear the imprint of her work. Rosalee was a member of the hymnal committee, and whenever a tune was found that needed a new harmonization or a more satisfactory musical arrangement, her skills were called into service.

Rosalee Smith Elser was born in Independence, Missouri, the first of two children of Rosamond and W. Wallace Smith. In due course, her father would become prophet-president of the church and would be succeeded by her brother, Wallace B. Smith. Music was highly valued in the home, and she says that from an early age she found herself "sitting on a piano or organ bench at home, in school, or at church." On Saturdays, the live opera broadcasts would be tuned in on the radio while the household chores were being carried out. Rosalee remembers:

> Mother used to play the piano almost every day, and would often sing from the hymnal. We would sing barbershop harmony on car trips and stand around the piano with family on holidays, taking turns choosing our favorite songs and carols. I loved to sing alto, or the tenor part "an octave up," in Sunday School, but fretted over some of the songs we had to sing and looked forward to the privilege of marching in a line upstairs from Junior Church to "grown-up" church on Communion Sunday, where we could sing from the *Saints' Hymnal*.

Rosalee attended Willamette University, Graceland College, and the Conservatory of Music at the University of

Missouri–Kansas City, where she studied piano, organ, and composition. She served for many years as staff organist at the Stone Church in Independence, and has developed a special interest in the area of new hymnody.

This hymn is a good example of the work Rosalee has done by taking existing folk songs and hymns and giving them harmonizations suitable for the hymnal. Of this particular American folk hymn, she says,

I was literally drawn into the seeming innocence of this hymn tune and text. The lyrics are simple and the melody easy and inviting. One senses, though, that the words and music...have risen from traditions and values where singing together was an act of simplicity and spirituality coming from deep within the soul. It was my intent to make the harmony rich in sound, and enjoyable to sing. This lovely hymn has the power to lift our souls to great heights through our worship in the service of Communion.

Another of Rosalee's harmonizations that is a particular favorite of hers is *HS* 125, "My Shepherd Will Supply My Need." That treatment of the Twenty-third Psalm is in the great tradition of English pastoral verse, and her musical arrangement is an effort to complement the sensitive text of Isaac Watts.

348 We Bring Our Children, Lord, to Thee
text by Evelyn Maples

This is another hymn written in response to a request by the committee that compiled *Hymns of the Saints*. The committee often found a dearth of hymns about certain subjects; this was particularly true of hymns about the ordinances and sacraments. Because of her experience in writing for and about children, Evelyn Maples (see *HS* 186) was asked to submit a text on the blessing of children. The author observes that her "years of writing for *Zion's Hope* and *Stepping Stones* [the church's publications for children] have helped me to feel especially close to the church's children." She has given us a hymn of celebration that expresses our deep appreciation for the precious gift of children in our midst. It challenges us to "each be parent, loving all," and asks for God's "timeless care" for each child.

The tune, by Henry Baker, was first called "Whitburn," probably after a small town on the North Sea near Sunderland, England. The name was changed to "Hesperus" (the name of the evening star) when it was used with the text, "Sun of my soul, thou Savior dear, it is not night if Thou be near."

349 The Vision of a Life to Be
text by Geoffrey F. Spencer
tune by Mary A. Bradford

In an effort to offer his own response to the scarcity of hymns on the ordinances, cited in the comments for *HS* 348, hymnal committee member Geoffrey Spencer (see *HS* 1 for more information) penned this text to be sung on the occasion of the blessing of children. The thoughts expressed are those that might be spoken in the elder's prayer of blessing but that can, through this hymn, be expressed together by the congregation. The corporate prayer is not for "sheltered ease" for the young life brought forward for a blessing, but for fortitude, eagerness, and courage. It is a prayer for congregational loving and caring, and it is also a prayer of blessing for all the "children of the earth."

The tune, "Gratefulness," was written by a member of the church in the last century, Mary Bradford. Additional information about the composer is given with *HS* 26, which shares this tune.

350 Baptized in Water
text by Naomi Russell, altered by Alan D. Tyree

Naomi Russell (see *HS* 150) wrote this hymn in response to the call for more hymns appropriate for the ordinance of baptism. The hymn is, in essence, the voice of the congregation speaking directly to the candidate for baptism. Alan Tyree (see *HS* 110) provided some of the ideas Naomi developed and also shared in working out some of the final wording. Thus the credits for this hymn show the names of both authors.

The Scottish composer of the tune, "Brother James' Air," was James Leith Macbeth Bain, affectionately known as "Brother James." He was a poet, mystical writer, and spiritual healer who formed the Brotherhood of Healers. He could often be found employing music therapy by singing to his patients in order to aid the healing process.

351 Redeeming Grace Has Touched Our Lives
text by Geoffrey F. Spencer

Again, Geoffrey Spencer (see *HS* 1) has given us a fresh, new expression of challenging thoughts concerning one of the sacraments of the church. This is a hymn eminently suitable not only for a service of baptism but for any service or moment of commitment. It expresses thanks for the gift of grace in our lives ("God's loving has pursued us") and for the nurturing fellowship of the Saints. It calls us to engage ourselves more fully in "witness to the risen Lord" through the remembrance of our baptismal covenant, our own hour of "dying and rising."

The tune, "Dominus Regit Me," was written in 1868 by John Bacchus Dykes for the hymn "The King of Love My Shepherd Is." A prolific writer of hymn tunes, Dykes was the minister at St. Oswald's Church in Durham, England, when this music was written.

357 My Lord, I Come This Hour to Make
text by William F. Webb

William Webb was born in Colorado and enjoyed life on the farm until moving to California for his high school years, which he says opened up new opportunities and new life viewpoints for him. He states: "It was my good fortune to associate with certain people at key points in my life that provided encouragement and leadership so that when opportunities came, I was in a position to accept and grow." After graduating from Graceland College and UCLA, he became an engineer. His career took him into the "high tech" world of machine design, where he had many interesting projects that involved extensive travel. He says that "lonely nights in a hotel room were often used to sort out rhymes and lyrics in a number of hymns which I would work on." Brother Webb has served in many offices and callings in the church, including youth leader and church school teacher, presiding elder, counselor to the stake president, and member of the stake high council. He now lives in Missouri, where he serves as an evangelist.

Brother Webb has borne the following testimony concerning his hymn:

Much of this hymn came out of my ministry as an evangelist and an attempt to put into words the special relationship between a person and our Creator in the making of a covenant through baptism. I tried to express my feeling of our utter dependence upon God and the extent of his love and of the intensive measures he has taken to establish his desired relationship with his creation. I was also thinking of the underlying meaning of this covenant and our feelings and thoughts as we enter into such a covenant. I must give credit to the power and ministry of the Holy Spirit at various times in this effort, because I have no other explanation for being able to assemble such meaningful words.

The melody used with this hymn has been arranged from a Norwegian folk song, "The Hardy Norseman's House of Yore," described as an ancient popular song "always sung with the greatest enthusiasm."

358 O God, to Us Be Present Here
text by Geoffrey F. Spencer

Geoffrey Spencer's contribution (see *HS* 1 for biographical information) to the church's limited repertoire of hymns for the ordinance of confirmation is once again a thoughtful poetic expression. With a sense of perspective and insight characteristic of its author, the hymn brings to our attention the symbolism of this ordinance in affirming our common commitment to the ideals of corporate unity and personal servanthood. The gift of the Holy Spirit is not sought for "privilege or gain," but for strength to share the "Lord's travail" and "grace to keep the faith."

The tune, "St. Matthew," first appeared in 1708 as a musical setting for Psalm 33. Its composer, William Croft, was successively organist at three different churches in London—St. Anne's (Soho), the Chapel Royal, and ultimately Westminster Abbey.

360 O Lord, We Come As Children All
text by Alan D. Tyree

Alan Tyree (see *HS* 110) has said that this hymn grew out of the concerns that he shared with the other members of the hymnal committee regarding the need for "more hymns for the sacraments of the church, baptism and confirmation especially." He states, "I attempted to think of the usual setting and personnel in a confirmation service, its purpose and implications, and this hymn resulted." The hymn reminds us that we all must come before the Lord as children. We are reminded of our baptismal covenant and offered the imagery of the very hand of God being placed beside the hands of the elders in confirmation, and that same hand being stretched out to us in an offer of divine guidance and love.

The text is wedded to a new tune, "Massachusetts," written by Katherine K. Davis in 1962 to be sung with the text, "From Thee All Skill and Science Flow." It is a melody of good inherent quality, but probably unfamiliar to many people. This case might serve to illustrate the point that texts on subjects that are appropriate to special occasions, and therefore not frequently used, might be sung more successfully if those planning the service would select a more familiar alternate tune from among those with the same meter (in this case C. M. D., or "Common Meter Double") listed in the hymnal's metrical index. This is easy to do if one will only sing the hymn through mentally to make sure that the tune actually fits the words in style and in placement of accents.

361 Behold, Thy Sons and Daughters, Lord
text by Parley P. Pratt
tune by Louise Hills Lewis

Only a month after his baptism in September 1830, Parley P. Pratt (see *HS* 206 for more information) was commanded, in Doctrine and Covenants 31, to join the group of missionaries who were sent westward to preach the gospel to the Indians in the frontier of Ohio. Pratt was so convinced of the divinity of the gospel and the Book of Mormon that he declared, "I would not at that time have exchanged the knowledge I then possessed for the legal title to all the beautiful farms, houses, villages, and property which passed in review before me on my journey through one of the most flourishing settlements of Western New York."

No doubt because of conviction such as this, the outcome of the mission to the West was the opening of the work in Kirtland. In only a few weeks, the number of converts in the area reportedly reached one thousand. The authors of *Stories of Our Hymns* believe that this hymn sprang from that successful mission:

It was [at] the close of a confirmation meeting that Parley P. Pratt's heart was touched by the sight of the confirming of many who had been recently baptized. Among this group were youth and age; unbroken families, sons and daughters with their parents.... It was a beautiful picture...[which] quickened his poetical imagery.... Thus the beginnings of the great work to be accomplished in Kirtland prompted this hymn.

The tune, "Confirmation," by Louise Hills Lewis, is also used with *HS* 354, "Here at the Water's Brink We Stand." Louise Lewis, a member of the church, also composed the tune, "Hills," which is used with "We Limit Not the Truth of God" (see *HS* 309).

362 A Diligent and Grateful Heart
text by Raymond Gunn

Raymond Gunn has been providing ministry on the local church level for many years. After graduating from Graceland College, he went on to receive bachelor's and master's degrees in music education. He taught instrumental music in Iowa and Missouri for thirty-eight years before retiring in 1988. Raymond attends the Blue Ridge Congregation in Independence where he is assistant to the presiding elder and ministers in a number of ways, including planning the worship services, playing the organ, and directing the hand bell choir.

Brother Gunn has shared his personal testimony concerning the writing of this hymn:

"A Diligent and Grateful Heart" was written during the summer of 1965. Franklyn Weddle had asked me to be on the staff for the church youth music camp at Graceland College. I was very anxious to be a part of this event, even though I had been having health problems. On the first Monday of camp I became quite ill and was forced to remain in my room. I began to feel sorry for myself and wondered why I was ill, away from home and loved ones, and unable to fulfill my assignment. Was this the Lord's will? Then a wonderful feeling came over me and I began to realize that instead of feeling despondent, I should be looking at all of the many blessings the Lord had given me.

As I contemplated the wonderful things happening in my life I felt the urge to write my thoughts down in a poetic form. The words flowed very easily because they were an expression of my innermost feelings. My health improved, and I was able to again resume my camp responsibilities the following day.

When I returned to Independence, I showed the poem to my wife, Alice. Although I did not think it good enough, she decided, without my knowledge, to submit the poem to the hymnal committee for their consideration. They accepted it and chose to use it as an ordination hymn, although it was originally written as an expression of thanksgiving for the joy of service.

This hymn has been well received by the church and can be successfully used in a variety of worship settings. The folk melody to which the text is set is a lovely tune eminently suited to congregational singing. It is said to be a "hymn of the ancient Irish church" and is named after the Irish saint who "carried the torch of Irish Christianity to Scotland."

363 According to the Gifts That God
text by Peter A. Judd

Peter Judd was born in Enfield, England, where he lived until age eighteen. He came to the United States to attend Graceland College, from which he received a bachelor's degree in religion and business administration. After graduate study in economics at the University of Kansas, he taught at Wayne State College in Nebraska for three years before moving to Independence, Missouri, in 1971 to accept full-time employment at church headquarters. Over the last twenty-four years he has served in the Christian Education Department, and successively as director of the Worship Office, Program Services Division, and Temple Worship Center. Peter has continued his formal study at Saint Paul School of Theology in Kansas City and has received the master of divinity and doctor of ministry degrees from that institution. He has written a number of books and articles for church publications. At the World Conference in April 1996 he was set apart as a member of the Council of Twelve Apostles.

Brother Judd has written the following account of the creation of this hymn:

> Toward the end of the process of selecting hymns for *Hymns of the Saints*, it became apparent to the committee (of which I was a member) that we needed more hymns that could be used at services in which the sacraments of the church are celebrated. I started thinking of the relationship between the call to priesthood, as represented in the sacrament of ordination, and the call to ministry shared by each member.
>
> I had long found the scripture, "All are called according to the gifts of God unto them" (Doctrine and Covenants 119:8b), to be particularly meaningful. So I tried to use the words of that scripture to create a hymn text. It took several rewrites and some suggestions from friends whose opinions I respect before the text was finalized. The last phrase of the first stanza contains some of the words I added that are not in the scripture. They contain what I believe to be the essence of the calling of all who would be disciples: to re-present the Son. The hyphen is important. We are called not just to represent Christ, but to re-present him. The use of the spelling 'intrusted' in the last stanza, rather than the more current "entrusted," is to remain faithful to the scriptural text.
>
> After I wrote the hymn and it was accepted for inclusion in *Hymns of the Saints*, it occurred to me that by omitting the second stanza the hymn could have wide application as a call to service in a more general sense to all people.

The tune, "Evan," was written by William Henry Havergal, a noted English minister and church musician. It was first published in 1847. His daughter, Frances Ridley Havergal, was the author of the hymn "Take My Life and Let It Be."

365 Lord God, We Meet in Jesus' Name
text by Kenneth L. McLaughlin
tune by Arthur Hicks Mills

Kenneth McLaughlin currently serves the church as a

member of the Council of Twelve Apostles. A native of Ohio, he graduated from Ohio State University with a bachelor's degree in education and a juris doctor degree from the College of Law. He received a master of arts in religion degree from Park College in 1992. Before accepting full-time ministerial responsibilities, he was assistant attorney general of Ohio, and before that he served as a staff executive in the church's Legal Services Division.

Brother McLaughlin recalls how he first began to develop a gift that he had taken for granted, for the purpose of making a contribution to the worship of the church. When he was first made aware of the need for new hymns for the forthcoming hymnal, he wondered if he could help. He says,

> I knew that I had the ability to create clever little sayings and poems, mostly of the kind to poke fun at friends or family. Without much thought or preparation, I could come up with phrases that rhymed and contained the right meter and syntax to be remembered. I suddenly realized that this gift of silly cleverness could be transformed to a gift of blessing for the church.

Brother McLaughlin continues, "I have taken very seriously the premise that hymn texts are one of the most important sources of theological instruction in our faith community." He says that in each of his hymn texts he has tried to "ensure that the texts reflect the best current thinking of the church in its expression as the body of Christ." This hymn, "Lord God, We Meet in Jesus' Name," was written in response to the need felt by the hymnal committee for more gender-neutral texts in the ordination section of the hymnal. It speaks of the gifts given to us through the grace of God, which find their ultimate expression through servant ministry.

The tune, "Hicks," was composed by a member of the Reorganized church, Arthur Hicks Mills (see *HS* 130).

369 Bear Each Other's Burdens
text by Barbara Howard

This hymn has found a particular resonance in the hearts of the people of the church, and it has quickly become one of the best-loved songs in the new collection. As is true with all good hymnody, it expresses thoughts uppermost in the hearts of many, and it expresses them more beautifully and meaningfully through the gift of poetry. The text is well matched to a poignant tune that, like most Welsh tunes, is best sung in four-part harmony in order to realize its full beauty.

Barbara Howard (see *HS* 58 for biographical information), while serving as a Herald House editor, was a member of the committee that compiled *Hymns of the Saints*. She has given the following testimony of the experience out of which this hymn came into being:

> "Bear Each Other's Burdens" was born out of two concerns. When I was in seminary I read about Martin Luther's use of hymns as a means of sharing scriptures. He wrote hymns for women and children who, in his day, were not taught to read, and in this way the power and beauty of scripture came alive for them. I wanted to see more of our choice Restoration scriptures put to music for congregational singing. The historical background and portions of Doctrine and Covenants Section 150 hold special meaning to me as does the text in Galatians 6:2.

One afternoon the hymnal committee reviewed the traditional Welsh hymn "All Poor Men and Humble," set to the tune "Olwen." That hymn was not accepted, but the tune was so beautiful that Barbara decided she would like to see it used in the new collection. She continues,

> I started jotting down favorite passages from the Doctrine and Covenants as phrases for a possible hymn. I took my notes home, reworked the stanzas and submitted them to the committee.
>
> My sojourn in the church has been with loving people who have borne my burdens and shared my suffering. The Galatians admonition to "bear one another's burdens and so fulfill the law of Christ" has enormous import for me. This hymn reflects my conviction.

386 Come Now, Sound the Call of Zion
text by Eric L. Selden
tune by Henry R. Mills

Like *HS* 314, this is a new hymn that expresses a broader vision of the cause and call of Zion. Eric Selden of Australia (see *HS* 183) wrote these lines in response to a need he felt to challenge young people to devote their energies to constructive efforts. The hymn was written, he says,

...at a time when our young people were very active in protest movements and marches here in Sydney as well as in other parts of the world.... But it had a wider application to needs the young people were blind to, and came out of the depths of my soul, as happens on rare occasions when I'm on a personal mountain-top.

This hymn expresses a challenge for Saints of all ages to build, on strong foundations, the vision of a future of high adventure with God in the redemption of the world.

The tune, "Pittsfield," was written by Henry Mills at the request of Mark Forscutt, who was looking for music with a marching spirit for the hymn, "God Is Marshalling His Army." Henry Richard Mills was born in 1844 near Kirtland, Ohio. Soon after the assassination of Joseph and Hyrum Smith, the family moved to Pittsfield, Illinois, where they eventually came in contact with the Reorganization. After going with his father to a preaching service held there by Mark Forscutt, Henry Mills was baptized. Following the death of his father, Henry succeeded him as pastor of the Pittsfield congregation. In 1884, the family joined with other church members who were gathering to Independence. There Henry Mills continued in the exercise of his ministry and became active in the music of both the church and the community. He was ordained a member of the high council of the newly organized Independence Stake in 1901.

As is noted in the discussions of other hymns, the Mills family has made an outstanding contribution to the hymnody of the Reorganization. One of Henry's sons, Arthur, is the composer of two hymn tunes, "James," used for *HS* 130 ("How Gentle God's Commands"), and "Hicks," used with both *HS* 3 ("With Thankful Hearts We Meet O Lord") and *HS* 365 ("Lord, God, We Meet in Jesus' Name"). His son, Frank, is the author of the hymn text, "Newborn of God" (*HS* 247).

387 O My People, Saith the Spirit
text by Joseph Luff

The words to this hymn, which originally comprised six stanzas, came as a prophetic message sung by Joseph Luff during a prayer service at the Stone Church in 1907. Through his wife's parents, Luff had been a convert to the Reorganization from the Methodist Church, where he had been preaching and giving consideration to entering the ministry. His conversion decision followed a rich experience as a recipient of the gift of prophecy and the gift of tongues.

In addition to the work of his ministry, Joseph Luff had obtained an M. D. degree, and in 1906 was named "physician to the church." At the time this hymn was presented, he was also a member of the Council of Twelve Apostles. For a number of years, the hymn was not printed officially, because it was the practice not to distribute prophetic messages for general use. In due time, however, it took its place as a revered part of the church's hymnody. There is a strong spirit of immediacy and urgency about this hymn, and it has always had a special place in the hearts of the Saints.

We sing this hymn to the same tune used by Joseph Luff, "My Redeemer" by James McGranahan. McGranahan composed many gospel hymns during his years as music leader for the nineteenth-century American evangelist, Major Daniel Whittle. This tune has a particularly interesting story. Major Whittle's first song leader, Philip Bliss, was tragically killed in a train accident in Ohio in 1876. Upon hearing of the death of his friend, McGranahan went at once to the site of the accident. He discovered in Bliss's trunk the text for a new hymn, "I Will Sing of My Redeemer." He immediately set to work composing music for this hymn and introduced it at the next service in Chicago, at which point he decided to dedicate himself to continuing the work and ministry of his departed friend. The popularity of this hymn was such that some thirty years later an RLDS apostle, Joseph Luff, would use it as the vehicle for an inspired message which has ministered to the church for nearly a century.

390 Hast Thou Heard It, O My Brother?
text by Roy A. Cheville

Roy Cheville (see *HS* 296) was one of the most prolific and able hymn writers the Restoration has ever produced. He has said that this hymn was inspired by Rudyard Kipling's poem, "The Explorer," which Cheville often quoted. Two of the key lines of this poem read as follows:

> Something hidden. Go and find it. Go and look behind the Ranges—
> Something lost behind the Ranges. Lost and waiting for you. Go!

Roy Cheville's own comments on this hymn are characteristic of the vitality he brought to his ministry:

> Here is a hymn for adventurous religion. It is a call to pioneers who are willing and wanting to dare with God. It is born of the conviction that healthy, dynamic faith always involves moving into frontier regions. It expresses the belief that we ought never consider that we have arrived at a finished goal....
> One who lives among college students senses the need to keep alive this adventurous spirit if youth of quality are to be attracted to the movement, and if their zestful spirits are going to be devoted to the church. They do not want a finished product with the spirit of adventure gone. They want a church that moves out into pioneering fields. We seemed to have no hymn that quite said this thing. So this inner something kept urging until the hymn was written....

The hymn has two forms of salutation: when one [person] speaks to another, the formal "thee" and "thou" are used; when God speaks ... the more personal "you" is employed to give the sense of the intimate invitation coming to each one.

The hymn is set to a strong tune that originally carried the heading "Air, Mozart" in a hymn collection of 1873, although no Mozart source has ever been located.

395 God of Creation
text by Naomi Russell

Naomi Russell (see *HS* 164) wrote this hymn at the request of the hymnal committee, who wanted to find a suitable text to go with this well-known tune by Handel. The music was originally written in 1746 for the chorus, "See the conquering hero comes," in his oratorio *Joshua*. Handel subsequently incorporated it in *Judas Maccabeus*, the oratorio with which it is most often associated.

The committee asked that Naomi's text be on the subject of world ecology, a theme being given much needed attention in our time. As one of the few hymns dealing so directly with this topic, it has found considerable use by the people of the church. It expresses the concept that we can become cocreators with God through the wise management of the bountiful resources he has first created. Because this text sets words or syllables to each eighth note of Handel's tune, it is best sung at a stately tempo so that each word is made clear.

397 All Things Are Thine
text by Roy A. Cheville

This hymn of stewardship was written by Roy Cheville (see *HS* 296) while he was campus minister and professor of religion at Graceland College. He has said of this hymn that it was an effort to express something of the concept of stewardship held by Latter Day Saints, inspired by the second paragraph of Section 101 of the Doctrine and Covenants:

> It is expedient that I, the Lord, should make every man accountable, as stewards over earthly blessings, which I have made and prepared for my creatures.
>
> I, the Lord, stretched out the heavens, and built the earth as a very handy work; and all things therein are mine; and it is my purpose to provide for my saints....

The hymn refers to Zion in the first stanza and attempts to integrate the concept of stewardship with the cause of Zion. Brother Cheville further explains that, in his hymn,

> Zion is interpreted in the light of God's timeless plan. It is not some celestial golden city of the hereafter but an achievement of good community through Saints working together with God, in a fellowship of mutual consideration.

The tune we use for this hymn, "Germany," first appeared in 1815 in a collection titled *Sacred Melodies*, in which the Englishman William Gardiner published a number of classic European melodies he had arranged for use as hymn tunes, a practice popular during the nineteenth century.

398 Let Us Give Praise to the God of Creation
text by Geoffrey F. Spencer

This is an important new hymn for the Restoration movement. Although it is placed in the section on stewardship, and it certainly makes reference to this concept, the text contains a great many other ideas that make it appropriate for use on any number of occasions. It is, in effect, a brief summary of Restoration theology. The author, Geoffrey Spencer (see *HS* 1) says that he might well have expanded this one text into several hymns. He explains,

Frequently in my contacts in the field, I would encounter the question, in one form or another, "What does the church believe today?" What I attempted to do here was to incorporate into the text what I believed to be foundational beliefs of the Restoration. With this in mind, I referred briefly to the concepts of: (1) restoration; (2) the living presence of divine power for the task; (3) the sacredness of all things; (4) the unity of spirit and element; (5) the ongoing search for truth; (6) men and women together in ministry; (7) the role of the church as sin-bearer; (8) the power of our heritage; and (9) the experience of the God who calls us into the future. In the course of working up the text, I found other ideas pressing for inclusion, or so it seemed, but resisted the temptation to add other stanzas.

The tune, "Wesley," was written by one of the most influential American musicians of the nineteenth century, Lowell Mason. In addition to his activities as an organist, conductor, and composer, he is best remembered for his encouragement of singing classes for children and his leadership in the establishment of music as part of the public school curriculum in America. This tune, written in 1833, is often associated with the text, "Hail to the Brightness of Zion's Glad Morning."

399 A Charge to Keep I Have
stanza 3 revised by Richard Howard

Richard Howard (see *HS* 58) has given us the following comments on his revision of this hymn by Charles Wesley.

I was guest minister at a youth gathering in 1977, and the theme song used there was this old favorite of many Latter Day Saints. I had never liked the third stanza of the hymn, because it seemed to be a denial of one of the central affirmations of the Christian faith: unconditional divine forgiveness of sin, no matter how grievous. I wanted the hymn, and this particular stanza, to declare in the most positive terms the breadth and depth of God's love for humankind. So, instead of "And on thyself rely, assured if I my trust betray I shall forever die," I substituted "And in thy grace believe, assured, forgiven, reconciled, thy boundless love receive."

The revision eventually found its way into the new hymnal. Further, by way of illustrating the effects of making changes to well-loved hymns, Brother Howard tells the story of an occasion when he was taking part in a service introducing *Hymns of the Saints*. While the congregation was leafing through the new book just before the meeting opened, an elderly gentleman raised his hand and asked, "What has happened to number 399? Don't we believe in the unpardonable sin anymore?" With his characteristic blend of humor and pointedness, Richard Howard replied, "Well brother, I guess we do, but we just don't have to sing about it anymore."

The tune, "Boylston," is another hymn tune by Lowell Mason, a leading nineteenth-century American musician and music educator (see also *HS* 398). He founded the Boston Academy of Music and was subsequently superintendent of music in the Boston public schools. Boylston is the name of a village in Massachusetts, and also a well-known street in Boston.

400 Source of All Gifts
text by Margaret Athey

Margaret Athey is a professional music educator who has spent most of her career with children. She was raised in Escatawpa, Mississippi, but she and her family have made their home in Overland Park, Kansas, for many years. She holds degrees from Graceland College, Indiana University, and the University of Missouri–Kansas City. Chief among her interests is church music and worship planning. She has served in a variety of leadership capacities in the church and has written for both music and church publications.

Margaret writes of the experience of creating this hymn of stewardship:

> In July 1978, our congregation was short of money. To meet the existing needs a certain Sunday in late August was designated as Sacrifice

Sunday, a day for sacrifice offerings. Our people were advised to prepare for this offering over a period of several weeks by praying and considering ways to create a true offering of real sacrifice. Some families gave up their regular weekly restaurant meals as their sacrifice contributions. Some gave proceeds from a garage sale; some children prepared for the offering by emptying piggy banks.

As a member of the worship commission I was helping to plan the service for the designated Sunday. We wanted to create a setting that would produce feelings of joy in giving as well as assurance of God's pleasure in seeing the sacrifices of the people. With all of this in mind, I began to search for a hymn which spoke to these things. The result was [the composition of] the hymn, "Source of All Gifts." It was constructed thoughtfully, prayerfully, and with many revisions along the way. I remember sitting outside at our patio table with a large tablet and pencil, deep in thought, scratching out words, and throwing page after crumpled page onto the ground before achieving any degree of satisfaction. The hymn was used effectively during our Sacrifice Service. I felt blessed in the writing and, later, in the singing.

The tune, "Mendon," named for a village in Massachusetts, appears in a number of nineteenth-century American hymnals, although it is referred to simply as a "German melody" whose source is unknown.

409 Touch Me, Lord, with Thy Spirit Eternal
text translated and adapted by Don C. Rawson

Don Rawson was born into an RLDS family in Michigan and moved to Missouri during his youth. After attending Graceland College and the University of Kansas, he spent two years in Europe, where he became particularly interested in Soviet affairs. Subsequently, he completed a doctorate in Russian history at the University of Washington. Since 1968 he has been on the history faculty at Iowa State University in Ames, Iowa, and has made several trips to the Soviet Union and post-Soviet Russia.

One of the best-loved new hymns in *Hymns of the Saints* has been the hymn, "Touch Me, Lord," with its spirit of deep devotion and its haunting Russian melody. The author has given this account of the creation of this hymn:

> As a professor of Russian history, I have long been interested in Russian religious culture, including the music of the Orthodox Church and of other denominations in Russia. During the 1970s, as the RLDS Church moved rapidly in expanding its international perspectives, I became impressed that one of the musical heritages from which our hymnody could benefit was the Russian tradition.
>
> Since congregational singing in Russia is found mostly in the Evangelical Christian groups, I searched their hymnals for works whose words carried a message of Christian dedication and whose music was uniquely Russian. Eventually, my choices narrowed to a particular hymn, which I felt spoke to our mission as a church. Because occasional passages in the hymn seemed somewhat archaic, I decided to adapt its central themes into English, rather than to translate the hymn exactly. A Russian pastor whom I consulted agreed that the adaptation preserved the essence of the original Russian text. The music is unaltered, retaining the minor key and extended phrasing typical of many Russian hymns. My hope was that this hymn would not only contribute to our appreciation of Russian religious music but also enhance our spiritual devotion.

417/418   From Isles and Continents Afar
text by Evan A. Fry
tunes by Franklyn S. Weddle (417)
and Louita Clothier (418)

Here is another hymn by the former radio minister of the church, Evan A. Fry (see *HS* 122). For many years, at the end of every World Conference, the appointee ministers would come up onto the rostrum after their assignments were read out and sing the old hymn, "I'll Go Where You Want Me to Go, Dear Lord." During the work on the 1956 hymnal, the committee agreed that the old tune to this hymn was no longer as appropriate as it might be. It was also suggested that there were many committed people who were called not to "go" but to "stay" for the often equally challenging work in home congregations. Brother Fry decided to see what he could do about the problem. He has written the following testimony of the creation of this hymn:

> As was my custom at that time, I arrived at my office adjacent to Franklyn Weddle's a little after seven in the morning, and after getting settled, turned my attention immediately to this hymn, thinking to see what I could do with it before anyone else arrived to disturb me. I think I can truthfully say that every hymn I have written—save this one—has cost me a considerable amount of work, study, revision, and rewriting. This one seemed to come without effort, and aside from a later change of the prepositions beginning lines one and three in the first stanza, required no revision or rewriting. When Brother Weddle came in shortly after eight o'clock, the completed poem was on his desk.

Evan Fry is said to have cited this hymn as his personal favorite of all those he wrote. Franklyn Weddle (see *HS* 291 for biographical information) subsequently wrote a tune for the hymn and showed it to Brother Fry, who proceded to sit down at the piano and work out the harmony.

HS 418 is a new musical setting for this hymn by Louita Clothier of Lamoni, Iowa. Her tune was originally written for a choral anthem based on Evan Fry's text. It has a freshness and breadth about it that serve to emphasize and enhance the inspired words of this hymn of commitment.

Louita Clothier has been involved with music all her adult life. She presently teaches stringed instruments in the Lamoni Community Schools and at Graceland College. She has acquired an international reputation as a teacher and teacher trainer in the Suzuki violin method. As a composer, she has written numerous choral works and orchestral works, some of which have been accepted by major publishing houses. Most of her compositions have been written for specific occasions within the fellowship of the church. The tune for *HS* 418 was named "Belsize Square," the location of the Clothier family's first residence after moving to London, England, in 1973.

431 O May Thy Church Build Bridges
 text by Evelyn Maples

432 If by Your Grace I Choose to Be
 text by Evelyn Maples

This pair of hymns appear side by side in the hymnal, and both were written by former Herald House copy editor Evelyn Maples (see *HS* 186). She says that, of her four new hymns in *Hymns of the Saints*, "If by Your Grace" is her personal favorite. The text was written for a specific worship service at Walnut Gardens Congregation in Independence, where the theme was to reflect the concept of self-worth. It is a beautiful expression of a profound idea that, through divine grace, we are all called to bring our God-given gifts into more perfect alignment with eternal purposes.

"O May Thy Church Build Bridges," *HS* 431, was written at the request of the hymnal committee. A poem from another source which contained a similar theme had been rejected by the committee, but the concept of the church as a builder of bridges from person to person seemed to be one that needed to be expressed. Evelyn responded with this text that, like *HS* 432, speaks of the worth of all persons and adds the effective imagery of the church spanning the chasms of pain, fear, and hate with bridges of love.

HS 431 is sung to the tune "St. Crispin" by George Elvey, who was an organist and choirmaster at St. George's Chapel in Windsor Castle, England. He also wrote the tune we use with the hymn "Crown Him with Many Crowns." The tune, "Mendon," used with *HS* 432, is discussed with *HS* 400.

434 When God Created Human Life
 text by Alan D. Tyree
 tune by William E. Butler

Several of the hymns of Alan Tyree (see *HS* 142) in *Hymns of the Saints* are based on scriptural texts and several are revisions of existing hymns. However, this hymn is one of three completely original texts he authored. It is a hymn that speaks eloquently of persons as cocreators with God, and of the divine gifts of love and grace as a sacred trust. Brother Tyree has shared the following testimony concerning the impact the writing of this hymn has had on him personally:

> I felt greatly inspired in writing this hymn. Like two or three others, it represents a distillation of the inspiration of an entire sermon into poetic form. I was deeply moved in writing it, and cannot either sing or read it, aloud or silently, without melting emotionally. It comes out of the center of my being, out of my personal "holy of holies," and is both too sacred and too much a part of me for me to be able to treat it as I would other less intimate or sacred things.

The tune, "St. Hylda," was written by an RLDS Church member in England. William Butler was born in 1889 and died in 1967, and was a lifelong member of the church's London congregation at Enfield. He was an amateur musician, largely self-taught, but music was a driving force in his life. He played in several British brass bands and sang in and directed numerous choirs. Composing religious music was one of his loves, and his output includes more than fifty hymn tunes, several sacred songs, organ music, and brass band compositions. This tune was written in 1914 and took first place in the Independence Music Club hymn contest of 1945.

436 Go Now Forth into the World
text by Kenneth L. McLaughlin
tune by Mark H. Forscutt

This hymn shares with *HS* 151 the historic tune "Emerald" by Mark Forscutt (see *HS* 24). The text was written by Kenneth McLaughlin (see *HS* 365) late in the process of compiling *Hymns of the Saints*. He states that it was written because of the desire of the committee to find appropriate texts for this particular tune. He says,

I easily recalled the tune from childhood, where it was sung in my grandparents' rural Appalachian congregation. I remembered what a grand old tune it was, but how antiquated the text "Burst, ye emerald gates" was. (This was even before I understood that texts and tunes could stand independently of one another.) When I sang the tune over and over again in my mind, I kept hearing a "missionary" zest to it. So I sat down and wrote a missional text.

Because its tune is stirring and its text articulates a strong sense of commitment to action, "Go Now Forth" has become a favorite with worship planners as a "sending forth" hymn.

441 In Nature's Voice We Hear You, Lord
text by Mildred Jordan

Mildred Jordan has always been interested in music and plays the piano and organ for services in the Houghton Lake, Michigan, congregation. As a result of her love for nature and her tradition of early morning walks, she began to write an inspirational column for the local newspaper. Her column, called "Early Morning Walks with Millicent," began twenty-five years ago and continues to this day.

Mildred shares the following story of the creation of this hymn:

In 1973 my husband and I attended a leadership workshop in Worship and the Arts. I took classes in writing from Evelyn Maples, and in hymn writing from Harold Neal. After a certain amount of instruction we were asked to try writing a hymn. Each participant sought out a more or less secluded spot to seek inspiration; mine was a bench in a quiet place.

I thought of the purpose of the workshop, of the various art forms that could enhance worship. As I thought, I prayed, and the words of this hymn came rather quickly as I wrote. I could see and feel what God expects of us: to develop our God-given gifts and fulfill His purpose in us.

The tune, "Ashland," is named for a street in Chicago where the composer, Keith Landis, grew up. Landis is an episcopal priest and musician who has more than fifty published hymn tunes to his credit.

454 Open My Eyes, O Lord
text by Roy A. Cheville

Someone has said that when they first looked at this hymn, they saw the phrase "new frontiers" and guessed that Roy Cheville must have written it. For Roy A. Cheville, religion was not a stuffy ritual or a dry academic discipline but an ongoing, pioneering adventure; this spirit of vitality is an important part of his legacy to the church.

This hymn was written on the Graceland College campus in 1939. The opening phrase was suggested to the author by the story of Elisha and the attack of the Syrians on his country. Brother Cheville explains:

> While Elisha's servant was afraid, the prophet sensed that around them were unseen forces of deliverance. So Elisha prayed, "Lord, I pray thee, open his eyes, that he may see" (II Kings 6:17). The prayer assumes that we live in the midst of spiritual resources that we do not even know exist, let alone realizing that we may tap them. It affirms that inspiration brings illumination.... [Inspired persons] see things and they see them differently.
>
> The second stanza reminds us of the saintly life as moving adventurously "on Zion's way." Each day, each turn or rise of the road brings new scenes. Saintly living becomes a discovery and an exploration.

The tune, "Bread of Life," was written in 1877 by the American musician, William Fisk Sherwin, a student of Lowell Mason in Boston. Sherwin taught vocal music in Massachusetts and New York and composed hymn tunes and carols for use in the Baptist Sunday schools. This tune is associated with the text, "Break Thou the Bread of Life."

455 O Lord, We Come in Gratitude
text by Cleo Hanthorne Moon

Cleo Hanthorne Moon grew up in Oklahoma, where she was a convert to the church at age ten. She attended Oklahoma College for Women and the University of Oklahoma, and later went on to complete a degree in library science at Columbia University in New York. After beginning a teaching career in Oklahoma, she moved to Iowa in 1930 for a teaching position at Lamoni High School. Five years later she joined the faculty of Graceland College, serving as English instructor and librarian.

Writing has always been a primary interest for Cleo Moon. Her first poem was written in the second grade. In 1945, in honor of Graceland's fiftieth anniversary, a collection of her poems about the college was published under the title *The Bell Tower's Eye*. Now in her retirement years, she is affectionately known as Graceland's "poet laureate." Her style is genuine and sincere, with a freshness of expression and a creative choice of words that stimulates thought.

This particular hymn is a prayer of thanksgiving and dedication (stanza 1), an expression of repentance and love (stanza 2), and a prayer for the strength and inspiration to serve and love completely. The beautiful tune to which it is sung was written by Albert Peace, who was an organist at Glasgow Cathedral in Scotland. The tune is most often associated with "O Love That Will Not Let Me Go," a hymn that has been referred to as "one of the most moving and profound hymns in the English language."

No less than five hymns in *Hymns of the Saints* are from the pen of this beloved poet. In addition to "O Lord, We Come in Gratitude" (found also in the *The Hymnal* of 1956), other hymns by Cleo Moon in the current hymnal include:

109 Here We Have Come, Dear Lord
   (also in the 1956 hymnal)

118 The Weight of Past and Fruitless Guilt
326 Leave We Now the Table of Our Lord
415 Help Us Express Your Love, O Lord

The first two of these are beautiful expressions of earnest repentance and the hope that can come through the grace of God and our own personal commitment. The third is a gentle hymn of sending forth from the uniting experience of the sacrament of the Lord's Supper. The last, another eloquent hymn of commitment, captures something of the warmth of the love of God, freely given, which must not be withheld from his world but shared freely with humankind.

459 Lord, Who Views All People Precious
text by Kenneth L. McLaughlin
tune by Henry R. Mills

When Kenneth McLaughlin (see *HS* 365) learned of the need for original hymns for *Hymns of the Saints*, he began work on a text that began "Lord, who views all people precious, worthy, lovely in your sight." As he wrote, he had the tune "Hyfrydol" in mind, although this was not to be the tune chosen by the committee. He says of the writing process:

I relied upon some of the theological study I had done in the advanced leadership studies offered to me as a staff executive. After many unsuccessful attempts, and with disconnected phrases rolling through my brain, I finally composed a three-verse text that I submitted to the selection committee. Frankly, I expected it to be rejected and gave no more thought to the matter. When the committee wrote back and asked me to make modifications in preparation for publication, I was dumbfounded.

This is a stirring hymn of commitment which sings of compassion, reconciliation, and the worth of all people in God's sight. The tune, "Pittsfield," was written by a member of the Reorganized church, Henry Richard Mills. It is discussed with *HS* 386.

471 When Holy Ghost Shall Come in Power
text by Evan A. Fry

Evan A. Fry had a strong sense of witness of the gospel of Christ. It inspired his years of ministry for the church and enriched those who listened to his testimony through the medium of radio (see *HS* 122 for more information on this author). He saw this medium as a tool whereby large numbers of people might hear the witness of the gospel message and be stirred to make it a part of their lives. This hymn carries the spirit of Christ's promise as recorded in Acts 1:8 (RSV): "You shall receive power when the Holy Spirit has come upon you, and you shall be my witnesses."

Brother Fry's hymn reaffirms the witness of the call of Zion. It is sung to a robust German hymn tune from the eighteenth century, first published in a German hymnal compiled for the chapel of the Duke of Württemberg.

472 Unto God, Who Knows Our Every Weakness
text by Albert McCullough
music arranged by Verna Schaar Gustavus

Here is a historic hymn of the church that grew out of the dedication of its young people. In the spring of 1921, the youth of Lamoni, Iowa, and Graceland College, under the leadership of Lamoni Stake President John Garver, organized an ambitious series of meetings in the old Brick Church. An orchestra accompanied the enthusiastic singing, and the sermons were delivered by Elbert A. Smith.

One young man unfortunately was unable to attend these services. Albert McCullough, a nineteen-year-old resident of Lamoni, had looked forward to this series of meetings for some time. However, since boyhood he had suffered from a condition which caused his bones to break easily, and on this occasion he was once again confined to his home with a broken leg. It was his custom to use these times of recuperation for reading and writing, and particularly for painting, for which he had developed considerable talent.

One afternoon during the week, several of Albert's friends stopped by to cheer him up and to tell him about the services. After a short time, one of them picked up a guitar and the group began to sing familiar songs. Among these was the Hawaiian song, "Aloha Oe." After they left, with this tune in his mind and frustration with his frailty in his heart, Albert began to write a poem, beginning with the words, "Unto God, who knows our every weakness, with faith we lift our hearts in prayer."

Two of the three stanzas and the chorus were written that evening, and during the final meeting of the week, George Anway presented them as a vocal solo to an appreciative congregation. It was the heartfelt prayer of a young man who sincerely desired to serve despite his physical limitations, and it has since been sung by thousands as an expression of faith and personal dedication. It has become known by the descriptive title, "Consecration."

The Hawaiian melody is still used with this hymn, in an arrangement by Verna Schaar Gustavus. Verna grew up in Michigan, where she began her first musical studies. After completing the public school music course at Graceland College, she began a career in music teaching, along with offering her musical abilities in service to the church. While at Graceland, she used her skills in musical composition to arrange the music not only for this hymn, but also for "Graceland Forever" and the Graceland "Alma Mater Hymn."

480 For All the Saints
revised text by Richard Clothier

Richard Clothier has been involved in music since childhood, and most of his life has been devoted to music and the arts at Graceland College. He has been a member of the Graceland music faculty since 1960, except for several years during which he had the opportunity to teach at The American School in London, England. He graduated as a music student from Graceland in 1955, and went on to receive additional degrees from three universities. He presently conducts the Graceland-Community Orchestra and serves as chair of the Graceland Division of Fine Arts and program director of the Shaw Center, the college's performing arts facility. He has served the church in various ways through music and as an assistant pastor, both in Independence, Missouri, where he grew up, and in Lamoni, where he presently serves on the stake high council.

One of the great historic hymns of Christianity is "For All the Saints Who from Their Labors Rest." The original text was written as a processional hymn in 1864 by the Anglican clergyman William Walsham How. For many years it was sung to a tune by the Victorian composer Sir Joseph Barnby. In 1906 a new tune was composed for it by the great English composer Ralph Vaughan Williams, the only world-class composer to have edited a major hymnal (see Part II). He wanted the tunes used with hymns to be examples of the best music possible. This tune has the unassuming name of "Sine Nomine" (literally, "without a name") but it nevertheless expresses something of the expansiveness and breadth of the God of time and eternity. It has been called "one of the finest hymn tunes of our century."

As a member of the hymnal committee for *Hymns of the Saints* until departing for London in 1973, Richard Clothier shared the desire of others on the committee to provide the church with fresh new hymnody. This was a period, not unlike the present, when the desire was being expressed for a shorter, less formal name for the church. At that time, the description "Saints" was being tried out in several contexts, such as the "Saints' Church" and the "Saints' Auditorium."

The author remembers:

One day at World Conference, as I listened to John Obetz playing the great hymn tune, "For All the Saints," I thought to myself, "This would be an excellent hymn for our church, if only someone would write new words which talk about *living* Saints, not dead ones." I tried the idea out on the hymnal committee and several other hymn writers, and they all thought it was a good one, but nothing came of it.

Although I am not a hymn writer by any stretch of the imagination, I decided that if anything was going to happen with "For All the Saints," I would have to work on it myself. So, I began to see what could be done, not by starting over entirely, but by altering the original hymn. There was a lot of archaic theology and language in the old hymn, and I decided to use only four of the original eight stanzas. As I worked, I found I really didn't have to change as much as I had thought and, in fact, had the remarkable experience of finding that the hymn practically wrote itself as I went along. And most remarkable of all, when I finished the last stanza, having changed the words, "Through gates of pearl stream in the countless hosts," to "From age to age resounds the countless host," I realized for the first time that the hymn now expressed a concept which had not even occurred to me in the beginning. It was now a hymn not only about *living* Saints, which is what I had set out to write, but, moreover, about the miraculous unity between saints throughout all of history and *latter-day* Saints.

I have not given very much to this hymn, but it has given a great deal to me. I will never forget the restoring, emotional experience the first time I heard it being sung. I was lying in a hospital bed in London, listening to a cassette recording brought to me by J. C. Stuart and T. Ed Barlow, who had just come from the 1976 World Conference. I had envisioned this hymn as a sort of "Battle Hymn of the Saints," and it ministers to me every time I sing it, whether in a small congregation or as part of the World Conference assembled.

Now, twenty years later, at the 1996 World Conference, there has come another experience with this hymn I will never forget. As President Grant McMurray was escorted down the center aisle to be ordained the seventh prophet-president of the church, the congregation rose and sang at the very tops of their voices, "For all the saints...Alleluia! Alleluia!" I do not believe I have ever heard such singing. And I thought, surely the future is assured for a people who can express in song such extraordinary zeal and devotion.

482 Let Us Breathe One Fervent Prayer
text by Joseph Smith III
tune by Norman W. Smith

Once again we have been blessed by the poetry of the prophet who accepted the leadership of the church after the death of his father, Joseph Smith Jr. (see *HS* 131). This hymn of benediction, which originally began with the words "Brethren, breathe one fervent prayer," speaks to the contemporary church about peace—the peace that is "the gift of God's best love." It challenges the congregation to go forward with "reverent purpose" and promises them the strength and help of the Holy Spirit as they do so. Those who would look with "chastened hearts" will see that the "clouds are silver lined! What assurance need we more?"

In his later years, "Brother Joseph" was to suffer the loss of his sight, but his mind remained clear and his faith strong. Upon his death in 1914, a perceptive editorial tribute in a Kansas City newspaper acknowleged the gift of revelation which can be the culmination of a life of saintly discipleship:

He was the Prophet, but first of all he was the Christian gentleman and the good citizen. As such he lived; as such he died; as such he will be remembered.... Kindly, cheerful, loyal to his own creed, tolerant of those of others, standing for modesty, simplicity, good citizenship, embodying in his private and public life all the virtues which adorn a character worthy of emulation, such is the revelation Joseph Smith leaves to the world, as the real interpretation of an ecclesiastical message translated into terms of human character.

This beloved hymn is again the fruit of the poetry of Joseph III set to music by his friend, Norman W. Smith (see *HS* 8 for further information on the composer).

490 Lord, Let Thy Blessing Rest
text by Joseph Smith III

Like *HS* 482, this is also a hymn of benediction and peace written by the prophet Joseph Smith III (see also *HS* 131 and 146). The text pronounces upon the congregation the blessings of peace—"the peace that Christ can give." Roy Cheville has given us the following apt comments, not only about this hymn, but about the theme of peace as revealed in the leadership of the prophet who was called "Joseph the Beloved":

> This is a benedictory prayer. It speaks the very heart of Joseph Smith (1832–1914). His was a gentle spirit who knew a kindly Father. After he was ordained president-prophet of the Reorganization in 1860, he went around to homes, congregations, and conferences with words of peace. At a conference at String Prairie, Iowa, June 1863, for example, he counseled the Saints, "We should preach the peaceable things of the kingdom." He kept reminding the members, the elders in particular, to live peaceably with their neighbors. At the same conference he said the elders should avoid "preaching so hard against the various denominations or otherwise pulling down the doctrine of the various sects, instead of building up our own." Likewise he advised Saints to be at peace among themselves. He was directed to say to the church in April, 1873, "Let contentions and quarrelings among you cease. Sustain each other in peace, and ye shall be blessed with my Spirit" (Doctrine and Covenants 117:13).

The tune, "Naomi," by Johann Nageli, is often associated with the hymn "Father, Whate'er of Earthly Bliss." It is one of the tunes brought back to America by Lowell Mason from a European trip. As is the case with this tune, Mason often turned to the Bible as a source of names for his many hymn tunes.

495 Now Let Our Hearts Within Us Burn
text by Geoffrey F. Spencer

This is Geoffrey Spencer's contribution (see *HS* 1) to the category of hymns on "sending forth." The author bears the following testimony of its creation:

This text was probably the easiest for me to write, in that the ideas emerged in what I felt was a natural sequence. As far as I can judge from my participation in congregations in the field, this has been one of the more frequently used of my texts, and one of the best sung.

As the material for the hymnal developed, I felt that a hymn of sending forth could be a positive addition. As with the majority of texts which I wrote, I had a particular tune in mind at the outset. In this case I believe there was a happy matching of text and tune. I wanted to evoke the feeling of excitement and courage which I myself have often felt at the conclusion of a strong worship experience—the moment of transition from the community at worship to the community in service. The idea for the text, and most of the wording, emerged during the closing service at a reunion where there was an unusually strong sense of commitment on the part of the people, and within a matter of minutes it was completed. It was the only hymn (with the exception of one whose authorship I shared with Alan Tyree) which I wrote down as the ideas came, and which needed almost no revision after the first writing.

The tune, from a Norse folk song, was arranged by William J. Kirkpatrick, editor of many gospel song collections.

497 With a Steadfast Faith
text by L. Wayne Updike

Wayne Updike has served the church for nearly all his adult life as a church appointee minister in work that has ranged from that of a bishop to that of a stake president. He has also served with specific responsibility for priesthood education throughout the church.

One night during a summer session at Graceland College in 1954, Franklyn Weddle was leading a discussion of the work on the forthcoming (1956) hymnal for the church. It was mentioned that there were many thoughts in some of the old hymns that had value but needed to be better expressed. One of the old *Zion's Praises* hymns cited as an example began with the phrase, "With a steadfast faith." Wayne Updike was listening to the discussion and was struck with that phrase and the need for it to be used in a "marching, shoulder-to-shoulder type of hymn."

Upon returning to his room, Brother Updike penned the first draft of this hymn; it has been included in both of the church's hymnals since, and has become a well-used hymn of commitment and sending forth. The concept of walking together with one another sharing the steadfastness of our faith is one that is ever new and ever needed. As we seek, in unity and love, the will and purposes of Divinity, the blessings and care of the Holy Spirit will be ours, and we will share in the life abundant.

The music with which we sing this hymn was written for Wayne Updike's text by Franklyn Weddle and Evan Fry, whose important contributions to the church are discussed with *HS* 291 and 122, respectively.

Postlude

Roy Cheville used to say that he could tell the spiritual vitality of a congregation by the way they sang. This statement has the ring of truth about it. Good congregational singing does not mean singing with professional, trained voices, but it does mean singing with enthusiasm. And it is generally true that when one sings with true conviction and an understanding of what is being sung, more satisfying singing (and even better music) naturally results.

It could also be argued that an important evidence of a vital church fellowship would be the quality and quantity of its original hymnody. Both fervent singing and prolific hymn writing have been hallmarks of the history of the Reorganized Church of Jesus Christ of Latter Day Saints. But there is evidence to suggest that these are areas that will provide challenges to the church of the present as well as the church of the future. In a recent article dealing with issues related to worship in modern society, I discussed a problem with today's entertainment culture, specifically,

...the audience mindset and spectator mentality that it tends to develop in all of us. We have become accustomed to sitting and watching as athletes or artists perform for us, and we may be forgetting how to be active participants.[*]

The testimonies of the preceding pages serve to call us to action. Many of these writers did not know they could produce hymns until they saw a need to be filled and stepped forward with prayer and dedication to offer whatever contribution they could. Geoffrey Spencer's comment that writing

---

[*] Richard Clothier, "Worship in an Entertainment Society," *Saints Herald* (October 1994): 13–14.

for him involves as much "perspiration" as inspiration is perhaps typical of all who endeavor to consecrate whatever gifts they have been given. The church has been richly blessed by such efforts.

In the process of compiling these testimonies, I visited with Cleo Moon, now in her ninth decade and a resident of a care facility in Lamoni. With her fading memory, she was unable to recall any of her hymns until we opened the book and read through them together. She was still able to appreciate the quality of the poetry, however, and remarked after reading each one, "I'm glad I wrote that then, because I couldn't do it now." My mind immediately went to the latter-day counsel of Divinity to work while it is yet day, for "the night will come when...opportunity to assist will have passed" (Doctrine and Covenants, Section 142).

As I leafed again through the pages of the completed manuscript, I realized how much I had learned from the many friends represented on these pages. I have learned something about openness to differing ideas from Dennis Aldridge, and about openness to inspiration from many, such as William Graves, Mark Forscutt, and Deam Ferris. I have learned something about dedication and perseverance from Charles Derry, and about enthusiasm and passion from W. W. Phelps and Parley P. Pratt. I have admired the gift of thoughtfulness of writers such as Alan Tyree and Barbara Higdon, and marveled at the unshakable faith of Joseph Smith III. And I stand in awe of the lifetime of devoted service of people like Evan Fry, Franklyn Weddle, and Roy Cheville. We would be truly blessed to learn the many lessons taught by the hymns of the Restoration, and by the lives of their writers. Herein lies not only the past, but also the future of a people who will seek to truly become the body of Christ and Saints of the latter days.

Smith, David H.	8, 312
Smith, Elbert A.	239
Smith, Frederick M.	316
Smith, Joseph III	131, 146, 482, 490
Smith, Vida E.	158
Snow, Eliza R.	140
Spencer, Geoffrey F.	1, 106, 151, 297, 299, 314, 349, 351, 358, 398, 495
Tyree, Alan D.	110, 142, 205, 206, 297, 301, 302, 350, 360, 434
Updike, L. Wayne	497
Webb, William F.	357
Weddle, Franklyn S.	291
Yamada, Hiroshi	230

Index of Authors and Translators
Hymns discussed in Part III

Author:	*Hymn numbers:*
Aldridge, Dennis	6
Athey, Margaret	400
Cheville, Roy A.	296, 390, 397, 454
Clothier, Richard	480
Coffman, Linda E.	199
Derry Charles	7, 26
Draper, Maurice L.	312
Ferris, Deam	298
Forscutt, Mark H.	2, 112
Fowler, William	307
Fry, Charles	332
Fry, Evan A.	122, 306, 417, 418, 471
Graves, William	53
Gunn, Raymond	362
Higdon, Barbara J.	69
Howard, Barbara	58, 369
Howard, Richard	58, 399
Jordan, Mildred	441
Judd, Peter A.	363
Luff, Joseph	387
Maples, Evelyn	186, 348, 431, 432
McCullough, Albert	472
McLaughlin, Kenneth L.	365, 436, 459
Mills, Frank W.	247
Moon, Cleo Hanthorne	455
Oakman, Arthur A.	292
Phelps, W. W.	33, 313
Pratt, Parley P.	206, 361
Rawson, Don C.	409
Robison, Pamela	241
Russell, Naomi	150, 164, 234, 334, 341, 350, 395
Selden, Eric L.	183, 386

Index of Composers and Arrangers
Hymns discussed in Part III

Composer:	*Hymn numbers:*
Anderson, Audentia Smith	158, 239
Booth, Frances Hurst	199
Bradford, Mary A.	26, 349
Butler, William	434
Church, Charles F., Jr.	306
Clothier, Louita	418
Elser, Rosalee Smith	342
Forscutt, Mark H.	24, 151, 436
Fry, Charles	332
Graves, William	53, 164
Gustavus, Verna Schaar	472
Lewis, Louise Hills	309, 361
Mills, Arthur Hicks	130, 365
Mills, Henry R.	386, 459
Neal, Harold	341
Rider, Dale	150
Robison, Pamela	241
Smith, Norman W.	8, 146, 482
Weddle, Franklyn S.	122, 291, 316, 417